THE
SECRET OF
GUIDANCE

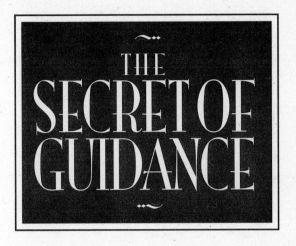

THE SECRET OF GUIDANCE

F. B. Meyer

MOODY PRESS

CHICAGO

Updated edition 1997 by
THE MOODY BIBLE INSTITUTE
OF CHICAGO

All Scripture quotations are taken from the King James
Version.

ISBN: 0–8024–6398-3

1 3 5 7 9 10 8 6 4 2

CONTENTS

1

THE SECRET OF GUIDANCE

Many children of God are so deeply exercised on the matter of guidance that it may be helpful to give a few suggestions as to knowing the way in which our Father would have us walk and the work He would have us do. The importance of the subject cannot be exaggerated; so much of our power and peace consist in knowing where God would have us be and in just being there.

The manna only falls where the cloudy pillar broods, but it is certain to be found on the sands that a few hours ago were glistening in the flashing light of the heavenly fire and that are now shadowed by the fleecy canopy of cloud. If we are precisely where our heavenly Father would have us be, we are perfectly sure that He will provide food and raiment and everything beside. When He sends His servants to Cherith, He will make even the ravens bring them food.

How much of our Christian work has been abortive because we have persisted in initiating it for ourselves, instead of ascertaining what God was doing and where He required our presence! We dream bright dreams of success. We try to command it. We call to our aid all kinds of expedients, questionable or otherwise. At last we turn back, disheartened and ashamed, like children who are torn and scratched by the brambles and soiled by the quagmire. None of this would have come about if only we had been, from the first, under God's unerring guidance. He might test us, but He would not allow us to fail.

Naturally, the child of God, longing to know his Father's will, turns to the sacred Book and refreshes his confidence by noticing how in all ages God has guided those who dared to trust Him up to the very hilt, but who at the time must have been as perplexed as we often are now. We know how Abraham left kindred and country and started, with no other guide than God, across the trackless desert to a land that he knew not. We know how for forty years the Israelites were led through the peninsula of Sinai, with its labyrinths of red sandstone and its wastes of sand. We know how Joshua, in entering the Land of Promise, was able to cope with the difficulties of an unknown region and to overcome great and warlike nations because he looked to the Captain of the Lord's hosts, who ever leads to victory. We know how, in the early church, the apostles were enabled to thread their way through the most difficult questions and to solve the most perplexing problems, laying down principles that will guide the church to the end of time; and this because it was revealed to them

as to what they should do and say, by the Holy
Spirit.

The Promises for Guidance
Are Unmistakable

Psalm 32:8: "I will instruct thee and teach
thee in the way which thou shalt go." This is
God's distinct assurance to those whose trans-
gressions are forgiven, and whose sins are covered, and who are more quick to notice the
least hint of His will than horse or mule are to
feel the bit.

Proverbs 3:6: "In all thy ways acknowledge
him, and he shall direct [or make plain] thy
paths." This is a sure word on which we may
rest, if only we fulfill the previous conditions of
trusting with all our heart and of not leaning to
our own understanding.

Isaiah 58:11: "The Lord shall guide thee
continually." It is impossible to think that He
could guide us at all if He did not guide us always. The greatest events of life revolve on the
smallest points, like the huge rocking-stones in
the west of England. A pebble may alter the
flow of a stream. The growth of a grain of mustard seed may determine the rainfall of a continent. Thus we are bidden to look for a guidance
that shall embrace the whole of life in all its
myriad necessities.

John 8:12: "I am the light of the world: he
that followeth me shall not walk in darkness,

but shall have the light of life." The reference here seems to be to the wilderness wanderings, and the Master promises to be to all faithful souls, in their pilgrimage to the City of God, what the cloudy pillar was to the children of Israel on their march to the Land of Promise.

These are but samples. The vault of Scripture is inlaid with thousands such, that glisten in their measure as the stars that guide the wanderer across the deep. Well may the prophet sum up the heritage of the servants of the Lord by saying of the Holy City, "All thy children shall be taught of the Lord; and great shall be the peace of thy children" (Isaiah 54:13).

And yet it may appear to some tried and timid hearts as if everyone mentioned in the Word of God was helped, but they are left without help. They seem to have stood before perplexing problems, face to face with life's mysteries, eagerly longing to know what to do, but no angel has come to tell them and no iron gate has opened to them in the prison-house of circumstances.

Some lay the blame on their own stupidity. Their minds are blunt and dull. They cannot catch God's meaning, which would be clear to others. They are so nervous of doing wrong that they cannot learn clearly what is right. "Who is blind, but my servant? or deaf, as my messenger that I sent? Who is blind as he that is perfect, and blind as the Lord's servant?" (Isaiah

42:19). Yet, how do we treat our children? One child is so bright-witted and so keen that a little hint is enough to indicate the way; another was born dull, and he cannot take in your meaning quickly. Do you only let the clever one know what you want? Will you not take the other upon your knee and make clear to him the directions that baffle? Does not the distress of the tiny child, who longs to know that he may immediately obey, weave an almost stronger bond than that which binds you to the rest? Oh, weary, perplexed, and stupid children! Believe in the great love of God, and cast yourselves upon it, sure that He will come down to your ignorance, and suit Himself to your needs, and will "gather the lambs with his arm, and carry them in his bosom, and shall *gently lead* those that are with young" (Isaiah 40:11).

There are certain practical directions that we must attend to in order that we may be led into the mind of the Lord.

Our Motives Must Be Pure

"When thine eye is single, thy whole body also is full of light" (Luke 11:34). You have been much in darkness lately, and perhaps this passage will point up the reason. Your eye has not been singly focused. There has been some obliquity of vision—a spiritual squint—and this has hindered you from discerning indications of God's will, which otherwise would have been as clear as noonday.

We must be very careful in judging our motives, searching them as the detectives at the doors of the English House of Commons search each stranger who enters. When by the grace of God we have been delivered from grosser forms of sin, we are still liable to the subtle working of self in our holiest and loveliest hours. It poisons our motives. It breathes decay on our fairest fruit-bearing. It whispers seductive flatteries into our pleased ears. It turns the spirit from its holy purpose as the masses of iron on ocean steamers deflect the needle of the compass from the pole.

So long as there is some thought of personal advantage, some idea of acquiring the praise and commendation of men, some aim at self-aggrandizement, it will be simply impossible to find out God's purpose concerning us. The door must be resolutely shut against all these if we would hear the still small voice. All cross-lights must be excluded if we would see the Urim and Thummim stones brighten with God's "Yes" or darken with His "No."

Ask the Holy Spirit to give you the single eye and to inspire in your heart one aim alone: that which animated our Lord and enabled Him to cry to the Father as He reviewed His life, "I have glorified thee on the earth." Let this be the watchword of our lives, "Glory to God in the highest." Then our "whole body therefore be full of light, having no part dark, . . . as when the bright shining of a candle doth give thee light" (Luke 11:36).

Our Will Must Be Surrendered

"My judgment is just; because I seek not mine own will, but the will of the Father which hath sent me" (John 5:30). This was the secret that Jesus not only practiced, but taught. In one form or another, He was constantly insisting on a surrendered will as the key to perfect knowledge. "If any man will do his will, he shall know" (John 7:17).

There is all the difference between a will that is extinguished and one that is surrendered. God does not demand that our wills should be crushed, like the sinews of a fakir's unused arms. He only asks that we should say "Yes" to Him. We ought to be as pliant to Him as the willow twig is to the practiced hand.

Many a time, as the steamer has neared the bank, have I watched the little lad take his place beneath the poop, with eye and ear fixed on the captain, waiting to shout each word he utters to the grimy engineers below; and often have I longed that my will should repeat as accurately and as promptly the words and will of God, that all the lower nature might obey.

It is for the lack of this subordination that we so often miss the guidance we seek. There is a secret controversy between our will and God's. And we shall never be right till we have let Him take, and break, and make. Oh! Do seek for that. If you cannot give, let Him take. If you are not willing, confess that you are willing to be made willing. Hand yourself over to Him to work in you, to will and to do of His own good pleasure. We must be as plastic clay, ready to take any shape that the great Potter may choose, so shall we be able to detect His guidance.

We Must Seek Information for Our Mind

This is certainly the next step. God has given us these wonderful faculties of brain-power, and He will not ignore them. In grace He does not cancel the action of any of His marvelous bestowments, but He uses them for the communication of His purposes and thoughts.

It is of the greatest importance, then, that we should feed our minds with facts, with reliable information, with the results of human experience, and (above all) with the teachings of the Word of God. It is a matter for the utmost admiration to notice how full the Bible is of biography and history, so that there is hardly a single crisis in our lives that may not be matched from those wondrous pages. There is no book like the Bible for casting a light on the dark landing of human life.

We have no need or right to run hither and thither to ask our friends what we ought to do;

but there is no harm in our taking pains to gather all reliable information, on which the flame of holy thought and consecrated purpose may feed and grow strong. It is for us ultimately to decide as God shall teach us, but His voice may come to us through the voice of sanctified common sense, acting on the materials we have collected. Of course at times God may bid us act against our reason, but these times are very exceptional; and then our duty will be so clear that there can be no mistake. But for the most part God will speak in the results of deliberate consideration, weighing and balancing the pros and cons.

When Peter was shut up in prison and could not possibly extricate himself, an angel was sent to do for him what he could not do for himself; but when they had passed through a street or two of the city, the angel left him to consider the matter for himself. Thus God treats us still. He will dictate a miraculous course by miraculous methods. But when the ordinary light of reason is adequate to the task, He will leave us to act as occasion may serve.

We Must Be Much in Prayer for Guidance

The Psalms are full of earnest pleading for clear direction: "Teach me thy way, O Lord, and lead me in a plain path, because of mine enemies" (Psalm 27:11). It is the law of our Father's house that His children shall ask for what they want. "If any of you lack wisdom, let him ask of God, that giveth to all men liberally, and upbraideth not" (James 1:5).

In a time of change and crisis, we need to be much in prayer, not only on our knees, but in that sweet form of inward prayer, in which the spirit is constantly offering itself up to God, asking to be shown His will; soliciting that His will may be impressed upon the surface of our spirit as the heavenly bodies photograph themselves on prepared paper. Wrapped in prayer like this, the trustful believer may tread the deck of the ocean steamer night after night, sure that He who points the stars in their courses will not fail to direct the soul that has no other aim than to do His will.

One good form of prayer at such a juncture is to ask that doors may be shut, that the way be closed, and that all enterprises that are not according to God's will may be arrested at their very beginning. Put the matter absolutely into God's hands from the outset, and He will not fail to shatter the project and defeat the aim that is not according to His holy will.

We Must Wait the Gradual Unfolding of God's Plan in Providence

God's impressions within and His Word without are always corroborated by His providence around, and we should quietly wait until these three focus into one point.

Sometimes it looks as if we are bound to act. Everyone says we must do something, and, indeed, things seem to have reached so desperate a pitch that we must. Behind are the Egyptians; right and left are inaccessible precipices; before is the sea. It is not easy at such times to stand still and see the salvation of God, but we must. When Saul compelled himself and offered sacrifice because he thought that Samuel was too late in coming, he made the great mistake of his life.

God may delay to come in the guise of His providence. There was delay before Sennacherib's host lay like withered leaves around the Holy City. There was delay before Jesus came walking on the sea in the early dawn or hastened to raise Lazarus. There was delay before the angel sped to Peter's side on the night before his expected martyrdom. God waits long enough to test patience of faith, but not a moment behind the extreme hour of need. "The vision is yet for an appointed time, but at the end it shall speak, and not lie: though it tarry, wait for it; because it will surely come, it will not tarry" (Habakkuk 2:3).

It is remarkable how God guides us by circumstances. At one moment the way may seem utterly blocked, and then shortly afterward some trivial incident occurs, which might not seem much to others, but which to the keen eye of faith speaks volumes. Sometimes these signs are repeated in different ways in answer to prayer. They are not haphazard results of chance, but the opening up of circumstances in the direction in which we should walk. And they begin to multiply as we advance toward our goal, just as lights do as we near a populous town when darting through the land by night express.

Sometimes men sigh for an angel to come to point them their way; that simply indicates that as yet the time has not come for them to move. If you do not know what you ought to do, stand still until you do. And when the time comes for action, circumstances, like glowworms, will sparkle along your path. You will become so sure that you are right, when God's three witnesses concur, that you could not be surer though an angel beckoned you on.

The circumstances of our daily life are to us an infallible indication of God's will when they concur with the inward promptings of the Spirit and with the Word of God. So long as they are stationary, wait. When you must act, they will open, and a way will be made through oceans and rivers, wastes and rocks.

We often make a great mistake, thinking that God is not guiding us at all, because we cannot see far in front. But this is not His method. He only undertakes that *the steps* of a good man should be ordered by the Lord. Not next year, but tomorrow. Not the next mile, but the next yard. Not the whole pattern, but the next stitch in the canvas. If you expect more than this, you will be disappointed and get back into the dark. But this will secure for you leading in the right way, as you will acknowledge when you review it from the hilltops of glory.

We cannot ponder too deeply the lessons of the cloud given in the exquisite picture-lesson on guidance (Numbers 9:15–23):

> And on the day that the tabernacle was reared up the cloud covered the tabernacle, namely, the tent of the testimony: and at even there was upon the tabernacle as it were the appearance of fire, until the morning. So it was alway: the cloud covered it by day, and the appearance of fire by night. And when the cloud was taken up from the tabernacle, then after that the children of Israel journeyed: and in the place where the cloud abode, there the children of Israel pitched their tents. At the commandment of the Lord the children of Israel journeyed, and at the commandment of the Lord they pitched: as long as the cloud abode upon the tabernacle they rested in their tents. And when the cloud tarried long upon the tabernacle many days, then the children of Israel kept the charge of the Lord, and journeyed not. And so it was, when the cloud was a few days upon the tabernacle; according to the commandment of the Lord they abode in their tents, and according to the commandment of the Lord they journeyed. And so it was, when the cloud abode from even unto the morning, and that the cloud was taken

up in the morning, then they journeyed: whether it was by day or by night that the cloud was taken up, they journeyed. Or whether it were two days, or a month, or a year, that the cloud tarried upon the tabernacle, remaining thereon, the children of Israel abode in their tents, and journeyed not: but when it was taken up, they journeyed. At the commandment of the Lord they rested in the tents, and at the commandment of the Lord they journeyed: they kept the charge of the Lord, at the commandment of the Lord by the hand of Moses.

Let us look high enough for guidance. Let us encourage our soul to wait only upon God till it is given. Let us cultivate that meekness that He will guide in judgment. Let us seek to be of quick understanding, that we may be apt to see the least sign of His will. Let us stand with girded loins and lighted lamps, that we may be prompt to obey. Blessed are those servants. They shall be led by a right way to the golden city of the saints.

Speaking for myself, after months of waiting and prayer, I have become absolutely sure of the guidance of my heavenly Father; and with the emphasis of personal experience, I would encourage each troubled and perplexed soul who may read these lines to wait patiently for the Lord until He clearly indicates His will.

2

WHERE AM I WRONG?

This is your eager question, O Christian soul, and your bitter complaint. On the faces and in the lives of others who are known to you, you have discerned a light, a joy, a power, which you envy with a desire that oppresses you, but for which you should thank God devoutly. It is well when we are dissatisfied with the low levels on which we have been wont to live and begin to ask the secret of a sweeter, nobler, more victorious life. The sleeper who turns restlessly is near awakening and will find that already the light of the morning is shining around the bed on which slumber has been indulged too long. "Awake thou that sleepest, and arise from the dead, and Christ shall give thee light" (Ephesians 5:14).

We must, however, remember that *temperaments differ*. Some seem born in the dark, and carry with them through life a hereditary predisposition to melancholy. Their nature is set to a minor key and responds most easily and naturally to depression. They look always on the dark side of things and in the bluest of skies discover the cloud no bigger than a man's hand.

Theirs is a shadowed pathway, where glints of sunshine strike feebly and with difficulty through the dark foliage above.

Such a temperament may be yours; and if it be, you never can expect to obtain the same exuberant gladness that comes to others, nor must you complain if you do not. This is the burden that your Savior's hands shaped for you, and you must carry it for Him, not complaining or parading it to the gaze of others or allowing it to master your steadfast and resolute spirit, but bearing it silently, and glorifying God amid all. But though it may be impossible to win the joyousness which comes to others, there may at least be rest, and victory, and serenity—heaven's best gifts to man.

We must remember, also, that *emotion is no true test of our spiritual state*. Rightness of heart often shows itself in gladness of heart, just as bodily health generally reveals itself in exuberant spirits. But it is not always so. In other words, absence of joy does not always prove that the heart is wrong. It may do so, but certainly not invariably. Perhaps the nervous system may have been overtaxed, as Elijah's was in the wilderness when, after the long strain of Carmel and his flight was over, he lay down upon the sand and asked to die—a request that God met, not with rebuke, but with food and sleep. Perhaps the Lord has withdrawn the light from your landscape in order to see whether

He was loved for Himself or merely for His gifts. Perhaps the discipline of life has culminated in a Gethsemane, where the bitter cup is being placed to the lips by a Father's hand, though only a Judas can be seen; and in the momentary anguish caused by the effort to renounce the will, it is only possible to lie upon the ground, with strong crying and tears, which the night wind bears to God. Under such circumstances as these, exuberant joy is out of place. Somber colors become the tried and suffering soul. High spirits would be as unbecoming here as gaiety in the home shadowed by death. Patience, courage, and faith are the suitable graces to be manifested at such times.

But, when allowance is made for all these, it is certain that many of us are culpably missing a blessedness that would make us radiant with the light of paradise; and the loss is attributable to some defect in our character that we shall do well to detect and make right.

Perhaps You Do Not Distinguish Between Your Standing and Your Experience

Our experiences are as fickle as April weather; now sunshine, now cloud; lights and shadows chasing each other over miles of heathery moor or foam-flecked sea. But our standing in Jesus changes not. It is like Himself—the same yesterday, today, and forever. It did not originate in us, but in His everlasting love, which, foreseeing all that we should be, loved us not-withstanding all. It has not been purchased by us, but by His precious blood, which pleads for us as mightily and successfully when we can hardly claim it as when our faith is most buoyant. It is not maintained by us, but by the Holy Spirit. If we have fled to Jesus for salvation, sheltering under Him, relying on Him, and trusting Him, as well as we may, though with many misgivings, then we are one with Him forever. We were one with Him in the grave; one with Him on the Easter morn; one with Him when He sat down at God's right hand. We are one with Him now as He stands in the light of His Father's smile, as the limbs of the swimmer are one with the head, though the head alone is encircled with the warm glory of the sun, while the arms and legs are hidden beneath the waves. And no doubt or depression can for a single moment affect or alter our acceptance with God through the blood of Jesus, which is an eternal fact.

You have not realized this, perhaps, but have thought that your standing in Jesus was affected by your changeful moods. As well might the fortune of a wealthy heiress be diminished or increased by the amount of her spending money. Our standing in Jesus is our invested capital. Our emotions at the best are but our spending money, which is ever passing through our pocket or purse, never exactly the same. Cease to consider how you feel, and build on the immovable rock of what Jesus is, and has done, and is doing, and will do for you, world without end.

Perhaps You Live Too Much in Your Feelings, Too Little in Your Will

We have no direct control over our feelings, but we have over our will. Our wills are ours, to make them God's. God does not hold us responsible for what we *feel,* but for what we *will.* In His sight we are not what we feel, but what we will. Let us, therefore, not live in the summerhouse of emotion, but in the central citadel of the will, wholly yielded and devoted to the will of God.

At the Table of the Lord, the soul is often suffused with holy emotion; the tides rise high, the tumultuous torrents of joy knock loudly against the floodgates as if to beat them down, and every element in the nature joins in the choral hymn of rapturous praise. But the morrow comes, and life has to be faced in the grimy countinghouse, the dingy shop, the noisy factory, the godless workroom. As the soul compares the joy of yesterday with the difficulty experienced in walking humbly with the Lord, it is inclined to question whether it is quite so devoted and consecrated as it was. But, at such a time, how fair a thing it is to remark that the will has not altered its position by a hair's breadth, and to look up and say: "My God, the spring tide of emotion has passed away like a summer brook; but in my heart of hearts, in my will, You know I am as devoted, as loyal, as desirous to be only for You, as in the blessed moment of unbroken retirement at Your feet."

This is an offering with which God is well pleased. And thus we may live a calm, peaceful life.

Perhaps You Have Disobeyed
Some Clear Command

Sometimes a soul comes to its spiritual adviser, speaking thus: "I have no conscious joy, and have had but little for years."

"Did you once have it?"

"Yes, for some time after my conversion to God."

"Are you conscious of having refused obedience to some distinct command, which came into your life, but from which you shrank?"

Then the face is cast down, and the eyes film with tears, and the answer comes with difficulty: "Yes, years ago I used to think that God required a certain thing of me; but I felt I could not do what He wished. I was uneasy for some time about it, but after a while it seemed to fade from my mind, and now it does not often trouble me."

"Ah, soul, that is where you went wrong, and you will never get right till you go right back through the weary years to the point where you dropped the thread of obedience and perform that one thing that God demanded of you so long ago, but on account of which you left the narrow track of implicit obedience."

Is not this the cause of depression to thousands of Christian people? They are God's children, but they are disobedient children. The Bible rings with one long demand for obedience. The key phrase of the book of Deuteronomy is, "Observe and Do." The burden of Christ's farewell discourse is, "If ye love me, keep my commandments." We must not question or reply or excuse ourselves. We must not pick and choose our way. We must not take some commands and reject others. We must not think that obedience in another direction will compensate for disobedience in some one particular. God gives one command at a time, borne in upon us, not in one way only, but in many; by this He tests us. If we obey in this, He will flood our soul with blessing and lead us forward into new paths and pastures. But if we refuse in this, we shall remain stagnant and waterlogged, make no progress in Christian experience, and lack both power and joy.

Perhaps You Are
Permitting Some Known Evil

When water is left to stand, the particles of silt betray themselves as they fall one by one to the bottom. So if you are quiet, you may become aware of the presence in your soul of permitted evil. Dare to consider it. Do not avoid the sight as the bankrupt man avoids his telltale ledgers, or as the tubercular patient the stethoscope. Compel yourself quietly to consider whatever evil the Spirit of God discovers to your soul. It may have lurked in the closets and cloisters of your being for years, suspected but unjudged. But whatever it be, and whatever its history, be sure that it has brought the shadow that is your daily sorrow over your life.

Does your will refuse to relinquish a practice or habit that is alien to the will of God?

Do you permit some secret sin to have its unhindered way in the house of your life?

Do your affections roam unrestrained after forbidden objects?

Do you cherish any resentment or hatred toward another, to whom you refuse to be reconciled?

Is there some injustice you refuse to forgive, some charge you refuse to pay, some wrong you refuse to confess?

Are you allowing something yourself that you would be the first to condemn in others, but that you argue may be permitted in your own case because of certain reasons with which you attempt to smother the remonstrances of conscience?

In some case the hindrance of conscious blessedness lies not in sins, but in *weights* that hang around the soul. Sin is that which is always and everywhere wrong; but a weight is anything that may hinder or impede the Christian life, without being positively sin. And thus a thing may be a weight to one that is not so to another. Each must be fully persuaded in his own mind. And whenever the soul is aware of its life being hindered by the presence of any one thing, then, however harmless in itself and however innocently permitted by others, there can be no alternative, but it must be cast aside as the garments of athletes who compete for the prize in wrestling or racing.

Perhaps You Look Too Much Inward on Self, Instead of Outward on the Lord Jesus

The healthiest people do not think about their health; the weak induce disease by morbid introspection. If you begin to count your heartbeats, you will disturb the rhythmic action of the heart. If you continually imagine a pain anywhere, you will produce it. And there are some true children of God who induce their own darkness by morbid self-scrutiny. They are always going back on themselves, analyzing their motives, reconsidering past acts of consecration, comparing themselves with themselves. In one form or another, self is the pivot of their life, even if it is a religious life. What but darkness can result from such a course? There are certainly times in our lives when we must look within and judge ourselves that we be not judged. But this is only done that we may turn with fuller purpose of heart to the Lord. And when once done, it needs not to be repeated. "Leaving the things behind" is the only safe motto. The question is not whether we did as well as we might, but whether we did as well as we could at the time.

We must not spend all our lives in cleaning our windows, or in considering whether they are clean, but in sunning ourselves in God's blessed light. That light will soon show us what needs to be cleansed away and will enable us to cleanse it with unerring accuracy. Our Lord Jesus is a perfect reservoir of everything the soul of man requires for a blessed and holy life. To make much of Him, to abide in Him, to draw from Him, to receive each moment from His fullness, is therefore the only condition of soul-health. But to be more concerned with self than with Him is like spending much time and thought over the senses of the body and never using them for the purpose of receiving impressions from the world outside. Look unto Jesus. "Delight thyself also in the Lord" (Psalm 37:4). "My soul, wait thou only upon God" (Psalm 62:5).

Perhaps You Spend Too Little Time
in Communion with God Through His Word

It is not necessary to make long prayers, but it is essential to be much alone with God, waiting at His door, hearkening for His voice, lingering in the garden of Scripture for the coming of the Lord God in the dawn or cool of the day. No number of meetings, no fellowship with Christian friends, no amount of Christian activity can compensate for the neglect of the still hour.

When you feel least inclined for it, there is most need to go into your closet with the door shut. Do for duty's sake what you cannot do as a pleasure, and you will find it becomes delightful. You can better thrive without nourishment than become happy or strong in Christian life without fellowship with God.

When you cannot pray for yourself, begin to pray for others. When your desires flag, take the Bible in hand and begin to turn each text into petition; or take up the tale of your mercies, and begin to translate each of them into praise. When the Bible itself becomes irksome, inquire whether you have not been spoiling your appetite by sweetmeats and renounce them; and believe that the Word is the wire along which the voice of God will certainly come to you if the heart is hushed and the attention fixed. "I will hear what God the Lord will speak" (Psalm 85:8).

More Christians than we can count are suffering from a lack of prayer and Bible study, and no revival is more to be desired than that of systematic private Bible study. There is no short and easy method of godliness that can dispense with this.

Perhaps You Have Never Given Yourself Entirely Over to the Mastership of the Lord Jesus

We are His by many ties and rights, but too few of us recognize His lordship. We are willing enough to take Him as Savior; we hesitate to make Him King. We forget that God has exalted Him to be Prince, as well as Savior. And the divine order is irreversible. Those who ignore the lordship of Jesus cannot build a strong or happy life.

Put the sun in its central throne, and all the motions of the planets assume a beautiful order. Put Jesus on the throne of your life, and all things fall into harmony and peace. Seek first the kingdom of God, and all things are yours. Consecration is the indispensable condition of blessedness.

So shall light break on your path, such as has not shone there for many days. Yea, "thy sun shall no more go down; neither shall thy moon withdraw itself: for the Lord shall be thine everlasting light, and the days of thy mourning shall be ended" (Isaiah 60:20).

3
THE SECRET OF
CHRIST'S INDWELLING

It is appropriate that the largest church in the greatest Gentile city in the world should be dedicated to the apostle Paul, for Gentiles are under a great obligation to him as the Apostle of the Gentiles. It is to him that we owe, under the Spirit of God, the unveiling of two great mysteries, which especially touch us as Gentiles.

The first of these, glorious as it is, we cannot now discuss, although it wrought a revolution when first preached and maintained by the apostle in the face of the most strenuous opposition. Till then, Gentiles were expected to become Jews before they were Christians, and to pass through the synagogue to the church. But Paul showed that this was not needful, and that Gentiles stood on the same level as Jews with respect to the privileges of the Gospel—fellow-heirs, fellow-members of the body, and fellow-partakers of the promise in Christ Jesus through the gospel (Ephesians 3:6).

The second, however, well deserves our further thought, for if only it could be realized by the children of God, they would begin to live after so divine a fashion as to still the enemy and avenger and to repeat in some small measure the life of Jesus on the earth.

The mystery is that *the Lord Jesus is willing to dwell within the Gentile heart*. That He should dwell in the heart of a child of Abraham was deemed a marvelous act of condescension; but that He should find a home in the heart of a Gentile was unbelievable. This mistake was, however, dissipated before the radiant revelation of truth made to him who, in his own judgment, was not fit to be called an apostle, because he had persecuted the church of God. God was pleased to make known through him "the riches of the glory of this mystery among the Gentiles; which is *Christ in you,* the hope of glory" (Colossians 1:27).

"Master, where dwellest thou?" they asked of old. And in reply Jesus led them from the crowded Jordan bank to the slight tent of woven willows where He temporarily lodged. But if we address the same question to Him now, He will point not to the high and lofty dome of heaven, not to the splendid structure of stone or marble, but to the happy spirit that loves, trusts, and obeys Him. "Behold," says He, "I stand at the door, and knock: if any man hear my voice, and open the door, I will come in to him." "We will come," He said, including His Father with Himself, "and make our abode with him." He promised to be within each believer as a tenant in a house as sap in the branch, as life blood and life energy in each member, however feeble, of the body.

The Mystery

Christ is in the believer. He indwells the heart by faith, as the sun indwells the lowliest flowers that unfurl their petals and bare their hearts to its beams. Not because we are good. Not because we are trying to be wholehearted in our consecration. Not because we keep Him by the tenacity of our love. But because we believe, and in believing, have thrown open all the doors and windows of nature. And He has come in.

He probably came in so quietly that we failed to detect His entrance. There was no footfall along the passage. The chime of the golden bells at the foot of His priestly robe did not betray Him. He stole in on the wing of the morning, or like the noiselessness with which nature arises from her winter's sleep and arrays herself in the robes that her Creator has prepared for her. But this is the way of Christ. He does not strive, or cry, or cause His voice to be heard. His tread is so light that it does not break bruised reeds. His breath is so soft that it can reillumine dying sparks. Do not be surprised, therefore, if you cannot tell the day or the hour when the Son of Man came to dwell within you. Only know that He has come. "Know ye not your own selves, how that Jesus Christ is in you, except ye be reprobates?" (2 Corinthians 13:5).

It is very wonderful. The heavens, even the heavens of heavens, with all their light and glory, alone seem worthy of Him. But even there He is not more at home than He is with the humble and contrite spirit that simply trusts in Him. In His early life, He said that the Father dwelt in Him so truly that the words He spoke and the works He did were not His own, but His Father's. And He desires to be in us as His Father was in Him, so that the outgoings of our life may be channels through which He, hidden within, may pour Himself forth upon men.

It is not generally recognized. That does not disprove it. We fail to recognize many things in ourselves and in nature around us that are nevertheless true. But there is a reason that many, whose natures are certainly the temple of Christ, remain ignorant of the presence of the wonderful Tenant who sojourns within. *He dwells so deep.* Below the life of the body, which is as the curtain of the tent; below the life of the soul, where thought and feeling, judgment and imagination, hope and love go to and fro, ministering as white-stoled priests in the holy place; below the play of light and shade, resolution and will, memory and hope, the perpetual ebb and flow of the tides of self-consciousness, there, through the Holy Spirit, Christ dwells, as of old the Shekinah dwelt in the Most Holy Place, closely shrouded from the view of man.

It is comparatively seldom that we go into these deeper departments of our being. We are content to live the superficial life of sense. We eat, we drink, we sleep. We give ourselves to enjoy the lust of the flesh, the lust of the eyes, and the pride of life. We fulfill the desires of the flesh and of the mind. Or we abandon ourselves to the pursuit of knowledge and culture, of science and art. We make short incursions into the realm of morals, that sense of right and wrong that is part of the makeup of men. But we have too slight an acquaintance with the deeper and more mysterious chamber of the spirit. This is why the majority of believers are so insensible of their divine and wonderful Resident, who makes the regenerated spirit His abode.

It is to be accepted by faith. We repeat here our constant mistake about the things of God. We try to feel them. If we feel them, we believe them; otherwise, we take no account of them. We reverse the divine order. We say *feeling,* FAITH, FACT. God says FACT, FAITH, *feeling.* With Him feeling is of small account—He only asks us to be willing to accept His own Word, and to cling to it because He has spoken it, in entire disregard of what we may feel.

I am distinctly told in Scripture that Christ, though He is on the throne in His ascended glory, is also within me by the Holy Spirit. I confess I do not feel Him there. Often amidst the assault of temptation or the fury of the storm that sweeps over the surface of my nature, I cannot detect His form or hear Him say, "It is I." But I dare to believe He is there; not without me, but within; not as a transient sojourner for a night, but as a perpetual inmate; not altered by my changes from earnestness to lethargy, from the summer of love to the winter of despondency, but always and unchangeably the same. And I say again and again, "Jesus, You are here. I am not worthy that You should abide under my roof; but You have come. Assert Yourself. Put down all rule, and authority, and power. Come out of Your secret chamber, and possess all that is within me, that it may bless Your holy name."

Catherine of Siena at one time spent three days in a solitary retreat, praying for a greater fullness and joy of the divine presence. Instead of this, it seemed as though legions of wicked spirits assailed her with blasphemous thoughts and evil suggestions. At length, a great light appeared to descend from above. The devils fled, and the Lord Jesus conversed with her. Catherine asked Him, "Lord, where wert Thou when my heart was so tormented?"

"I was in thy heart," He answered.

"O Lord, Thou art everlasting truth," she replied, "and I humbly bow before Thy word; but how can I believe that Thou wast in my heart when it was filled with such detestable thoughts?"

"Did these thoughts give thee pleasure or pain?" He asked.

"An exceeding pain and sadness," was her reply.

The Lord said, "Thou wast in woe and sadness because I was in the midst of thy heart. My presence it was which rendered those thoughts insupportable to thee. When the period I had determined for the duration of the combat had elapsed, I sent forth the beams of My light, and the shades of hell were dispelled, because they cannot resist that light."

The Glory of This Mystery

When God's secrets break open, they do so in glory. The wealth of the root hidden in the ground is revealed in the hues of orchid or scent of rose. The hidden beauty of a beam of light is unraveled in the sevenfold color of the rainbow. The swarming, infinitesimal life of southern seas breaks into waves of phosphorescence when cleft by the keel of the ship. And whenever the unseen world has revealed itself to mortal eyes, it has been in glory. It was especially so at the Transfiguration, when the Lord's nature broke from the strong restraint within which He had confined it and revealed itself to the eye of man. "His face did shine as the sun, and his raiment was white as the light" (Matthew 17:2).

So when we accept the fact of His existence deeper within us than our own and make it one of the aims of our life to draw on it and develop it, we shall be conscious of a glory transfiguring our life and irradiating ordinary things, which will make earth, with its commonest engagements, like the vestibule of heaven.

The wife of Jonathan Edwards had been the subject of great fluctuations in religious experience and frequent depression till she came to the point of renouncing the world and yielding herself up to be possessed by these mighty truths. But as soon as this was the case, a marvelous change took place. She began to experience a constant, uninterrupted rest; sweet peace and serenity of soul; a continual rejoicing in all the works of God's hands, whether of nature or of daily providence; a wonderful access to God by prayer, as it were seeing Him and immediately conversing with Him; all tears wiped away; all former troubles and sorrows of life forgotten, except grief for past sins and for the dishonor done to Christ in the world; a daily sensible doing and suffering everything for God and doing all with a continual uninterrupted cheerfulness, peace, and joy.

Such glory—the certain pledge of the glory to be revealed—is within reach of each reader of these lines who will dare day by day to reckon that Christ lives within and will be content to die to the energies and prompting for the self-life so that there may be room for the Christ-life to reveal itself. "I am crucified with Christ," said the greatest human teacher of this divine art; "Christ liveth in me . . . I live by the faith of the Son of God" (Galatians 2:20).

The Riches of the Glory of This Mystery

When this mystery or secret of the divine life in man is apprehended and made use of, it gives great wealth to life. If all the treasures of wisdom, knowledge, power, and grace reside in Jesus, and He has become the cherished and honored resident of our nature, it is clear that we also must be greatly enriched. It is like a poor man having a millionaire friend come to live with him.

There are riches of patience. Life is not easy to any of us. No branch escapes the pruning knife; no jewel the wheel; no child the rod. People tyrannize and vex us almost beyond endurance. Circumstances strain us till the chords of our hearts threaten to snap. Our nervous system is overtaxed by the rush and competition of our times. Indeed, we have need of patience.

Never to relax the self-watch; never to indulge in unkind or thoughtless criticism of others; never to utter the hasty word or permit the sharp retort; never to complain except to God; never to permit hard and distrustful thoughts to lodge within the soul; to be always more thoughtful of others than self; to detect the one blue spot in the clouded sky; to be on the alert to find an excuse for those who are forward and awkward; to suffer the aches and pains, the privations and trials of life, sweetly, submissively, trustfully; to drink the bitter cup, with the eye fixed on the Father's face, without a murmur or complaint: this needs patience, which mere stoicism could never give.

And we cannot live such a life till we have learned to avail ourselves of the riches of the indwelling Christ. The beloved apostle speaks of being a partaker of the patience which is in Jesus (Revelation 1:9). So may we be. That calm, unmurmuring, unreviling patience, which made the Lamb of God dumb before His shearers, is ours.

Robert Hall was once overheard saying amid the heat of an argument, "Calm me, O Lamb of God!"

But we may go further and say, "Lord Jesus, let Your patience arise in me, as a spring of fresh water in a briny sea."

There are riches of grace. Alone among the great cities of the world, Jerusalem had no river. But the glorious Lord was in the midst of her, and He became a place of broad rivers and streams, supplying from Himself all that rivers gave to cities, at the foot of whose walls the welcome water lapped.

This is a picture of what we have, who dare to reckon on the indwelling of our glorious

Lord, as King, Lawgiver, and Savior. He makes all grace to abound toward us so that we have a sufficiency for all emergencies and can abound in every good work. In His strength, ever rising up within us, we are able to do as much as those who are endowed with the greatest mental and natural gifts, and we escape the temptations to vainglory and pride by which they are beset.

The grace of purity and self-control, of fervent prayer and understanding in the Scriptures, of love for men and zeal for God, of lowliness and meekness, of gentleness and goodness—all is in Christ; and if Christ is in us, all is ours also. Oh, that we would dare to believe it, and draw on it, letting down the pitcher of faith into the deep well of Christ's indwelling, opened within us by the Holy Spirit!

It is impossible, in these brief limits, to elaborate further this wonderful thought. But if only we would meet every call, difficulty, and trial, *not* saying, as we so often do, "I shall never be able to go through it," but saying, "I cannot; but Christ is in me, and He can," we should find that all trials were intended to reveal and unfold the wealth hidden within us, until Christ was formed within us and His life manifested in our mortal body (Colossians 1:27). How do we become more conscious of His life within us?

1. Be still each day for a short time, sitting before God in meditation, and ask the Holy

Spirit to reveal to you the truth of Christ's indwelling. Ask God to be pleased to make known to you what is the riches of the glory of this mystery (Colossians 1:27).

2. Reverence your nature as the temple of the indwelling Lord. As the Easterner bares his feet, and the Westerner his head, on entering the limit of a temple, so be very careful of anything that would defile the body or soil the soul. No beasts must be herded in the temple courts. Get Christ to drive them out. "Know ye not that ye are the temple of God? . . . The temple of God is holy, which ye are" (1 Corinthians 3:16–17).

3. Hate your own life. "If any man . . . hate . . . not his own life," said our Lord, "he cannot be my disciple" (Luke 14:26). And the word translated "life" is *soul,* the seat and center of the self-life with its restless energies and activities, its choices and decisions, its ceaseless strivings at independence and leadership. This is the greatest hindrance to our enjoyment of the indwelling Christ. If we will acquire the habit of saying no not only to our bad but to our good self; if we will daily deliver ourselves up to death for Jesus' sake; if we will take up our cross and follow the Master, though it be to His grave, we shall become increasingly conscious of being possessed by a richer, deeper, more divine life than our own.

4

FACT, FAITH, AND FEELING

These three words stand for three important factors in character and life. We all have to deal with them in one form or another, but it is above all things necessary that we should place them in the right order.

Most people try to put *feeling* first, with as much success as if they tried to build the top story of a house before laying its foundations. Their order is

FEELING,		FEELING,
FACT,	or	FAITH,
FAITH.		FACT.

Others seek *faith* first, without considering the facts on which alone faith and feeling can rest. They resemble the man who, desiring to get warm on a frosty night, refuses to approach the fire that burns brightly on the hearth.

The only possible order that will bring blessing and comfort to the heart is that indicated in our title:

God's *facts,* laid like a foundation of adamant.

Our *faith,* apprehending and resting on them.

Joyous *feelings,* coming all at once or after the lapse of days and months, as God wills.

Fact

The facts of which we are told in the Bible are like stepping-stones across a brook. Before you reach the shallows where they lie, you wonder how you will get over, but when you step down to the margin of the water, you see that they span the space from bank to bank. When you have reached one you can step to another, and so get across. It is absurd to consult feeling, or look for faith, while still at a distance from the brookside, or to persist in going above or below that primitive bridge of stones. You must come down to them, consider them, see how strongly fixed they are in the oozy bed, notice how easily the villagers pass and repass; *then* you will feel able to trust them, and finally, with a light heart and great sense of relief, step from one to another.

Let us recall a few facts that may help us first to faith, and then to feeling.

It is a fact that God loves each of us with the tenderest and most particular love. You may not believe or feel it; the warm summer sun may be shining against your shuttered and curtained window without making itself seen or felt within; but your failure to realize and appreciate the fact of God's love toward you cannot alter its being so.

It is a fact that in Jesus every obstacle has been removed out of the way of your immediate forgiveness and acceptance. God was in the dying Savior, putting away sin, bearing our sins in His own body on the tree, reconciling the world to Himself. You may not believe this, or feel the joy of it, but that does not alter the fact that it is so.

After the peace was signed between the North and the South, ending the Civil War, there were soldiers hiding in the woods, barely surviving on berries, who might have returned to their homes. They either did not know, or did not believe, the good news, and they went on starving long after their comrades had been welcomed by their wives and children. Theirs was the loss, but their failure in knowledge or belief did not alter the fact that peace was proclaimed and that the door was wide open for their return.

A friend may have paid all my debts in my native town, from which I have fled fearing arrest and disgrace. He may have done it so speedily that my credit has never been impaired or my good name forfeited. There may be all the old love and honor waiting to greet me. He may have even told me so; but if I still absent myself, and refuse to return, my folly in this respect cannot undo those beneficent acts, though it perpetuates my misery.

It is a fact that the moment a person trusts Christ, he is born into God's family and becomes a child of God. There is no doubt about this. You may not feel good, or earnest, or anxious; you may even be conscious of recent failure. You may be spending your days under a pall of somber depression, but if you have received Christ, and have truly trusted in Him, you have been born again, not of man, nor of the will of the flesh, but of God (John 1:13). You may be a prodigal or inconsistent child, but you are a child. If you were wise you would take the child's place at the Father's table and enjoy His smiles. They await you. But if you still remain out in the cold, as the elder brother in the parable did, you do not alter the fact that your place is ready for you to occupy when you will.

It is a fact that God takes what we give, and as soon as we give it. There is no long interval. When we let go, He receives. When we place ourselves on His altar, we are immediately sealed as His. When we consecrate ourselves, He accepts. The divine act is instantaneous. You may not be aware of this, and you may continue giving yourself day after day. If you do, you burden yourself with needless anxiety; you continue offering what is not now yours to give, and you lose the blessedness of realizing what it is to be the absolute property, chattel, and slave of the blessed Master. But your mistake cannot alter the fact that God took you at your word when first you gave yourself over to Him in a solemn act of dedication. Shall our lack of faith make of no effect the faithfulness of God?

It is a fact that in Jesus Christ we are seated in heavenly places. We cannot alter this. We may not believe it, avail ourselves of all the privileges it implies, or enjoy the blessedness of nearness to Jesus; but such is, nevertheless, our rightful position in the divine order. If we are united with Jesus by the slenderest strand of faith, we are as much one with Him as the loftiest saints; and where the Head is, there is also the Body. In Him we died on the cross and so met the righteous demands of the holy law. In Him we lay in the grave, and so passed out of the region ruled by the prince of the power of the air. In Him we rose and ascended far above all might and dominion, principality and power.

Is Satan under Christ's feet? In God's purpose, he is under ours also. Are death and the grave forever behind Christ? So, in God's purpose, we have passed to the Easter side of them both and are to the windward of the storm. As far as their sting or terror is concerned, they are like the Egyptians, dead on the seashore. Has the great High Priest passed through the heavens within the veil? So, in the purpose of God, we too have passed from the outer court into the Holy Place, where we offer gifts, sacrifices, supplications, and intercessions for all men.

All this may appear unreal and impossible, and the poor Cinderella's idea of being the bride of a prince, but it is nevertheless our true position. These are the facts of the eternal world, whether you avail yourself of them or not. There are not a few cases on record of former slaves starving in bondage because they would not avail themselves of freedom and of noblemen living a hard and difficult life because they would not claim their rights.

It is a fact that there is a share in the gift of Pentecost waiting for each member of Christ. To each one grace has been given. The promise of the Holy Spirit is to as many as the Lord our God shall call. Without doubt you have a share in that infilling, that divine unction, that marvelous power in service, which transformed the apostles from being timid sheep to lions in fight. You may never have put in your claim, but there is no grace that others have that you may not obtain. All things are yours. God has made over to you the unsearchable riches of Christ. Eye has not seen, nor ear heard, nor the heart of man conceived, all the stores of grace and love and power that are yours in Christ, accumulated for you in the Divine Deposit Bank. It seems a thousand pities that you should live a beggar's life when such wealth and power are yours, but if you persist in doing so, your folly and blindness do not alter the fact that the fullness of God is yours in Christ.

These are some of those facts, made known to us in the Word of God, that will conduct us over the brook of turbid emotion to firm standing ground. Let us give up worrying about our faith, or feeling the pulse of emotion, and come to rest on them, assured that they are more stable than heaven or earth.

Faith

If you want a true faith, do not think about it, but look away to the facts of which we have been speaking. We find no difficulty in trusting our friends, because we open our heart, like south windows, to their love. We recall all their interpositions on our behalf. We remember all they have promised and performed. Where would be our difficulty about faith if we ceased worrying about it and were occupied with the object of faith—Jesus Christ our Lord?

Faith is more than creed. In a creed we believe about a person or circumstance, but in faith we repose our trust *upon* a person. We must not believe about Christ only, but in Him, as Livingstone did, when on one occasion he was opposed at nightfall by an army of infuriated savages and was tempted to steal away in the dark. Then his eye lit on the promise, "I will be with you all the days." He wrote, "I went to sleep because I knew it was the word of a perfect gentleman." Do not believe about Christ, but in Him.

Faith concerns itself with a person. We are saved and blessed by the faith that passes beyond the fact of our Savior's life to Himself. We rest not on the atonement, but on Him who made it; not on the death, but on Him who died; not on the resurrection, but on Him who rose, ascended, and ever lives to make intercession; not in statements about Him, but in Him of whom they are made.

Many a time the question is asked by the inquirer, "Have I the right kind of faith?" It is a needful question, because there is a dead and spurious faith that will fail us in the supreme crisis, as the badly canned meats did an Arctic exploration party, who, on returning to their heap of stores, found them useless, and starved.

There is one simple reply, "All faith that turns toward Jesus is the right faith." It may bring no conscious rapture. It may be as weak as the woman's touch on His garment's hem. It may be as small and insignificant as a grain of mustard seed. It may be as despairing as Peter's cry, "Lord, save, or I perish!" But if its deepest yearning be Christ—Christ—Christ, it is the tiny thread that will bring the lost soul through subterranean passages, in which it had been well-nigh overwhelmed, into the light of life.

True faith reckons on God's faithfulness. In earlier life I used to seek after greater faith by considering how great God was, how rich, how strong; why should He not give me money for

His work, since He was so rich? Why not carry the entire burden of my responsibilities, since He was so mighty? These considerations helped me less, however, than my now certain conviction that He is absolutely faithful; faithful to His covenant engagements in Christ, faithful to His promises, and faithful to the soul that at His clear call has stepped out into any enterprise for Him. We may lose heart and hope, our head may turn dizzy and our heart faint, lover and friend may stand at a distance, the mocking voices of our foes may suggest that God has forgotten or forsaken; but He abideth faithful. He cannot deny Himself; He cannot disown the helpless child whom He has begotten; He cannot throw aside responsibilities He has assumed. He has made, and He must bear.

Often I have gone to God in dire need, aggravated by nervous depression and heartsickness, and said, "My faith is flickering out. Its hand seems paralyzed, its eye blinded, its old glad song silenced forever. But You are faithful, and I am reckoning on You!" The soul loves to go behind the promises of God to Himself who made them, as the wife needs not quote the pledges made by her husband in the marriage service when she is sure of him and feels the pressure of his hand.

Do not trouble about your faith; reckon on God's faithfulness. If He bids you step out onto the water, He knows that He can bring you safely back to the boat. When an Alpine guide takes you over a ragged piece of ice, he considers whether, in the event of your utter collapse, he is able to carry you through by the strength of his iron grasp and sinewy frame. What iron is to the blood, the thought of God's faithfulness is to faith. "Sarah . . . received strength to conceive . . . because she judged him faithful who had promised" (Hebrews 11:11); Abraham "was strong in faith, giving glory to God" (Romans 4:20).

Faith bears fruit. It cannot help it, because faith links the soul with Christ, so that the energy of His life pours into the soul through the artery of faith, and, as it comes in, so it must make a way out for itself. Fruit is (so to speak) forced from the believing soul. Why does the lark sing? It cannot help it, because the spirit of spring has been poured into its heart. Why does the branch bear fruit? It cannot help it, because the life-forces are ever pouring up from the root. Why does a child run to meet his mother? He cannot help it, because his heart has imbibed her nature. So the believer, united in Christ, receives grace upon grace from His heart, and from the abundance of His indwelling the believer's life speaks.

It is not difficult to obtain faith like this. Put your will on the side of Christ—not a passing wish, but the whole desire and choice of your being. Be willing to believe; or be willing to be made willing to believe. Lift your eyes toward Christ. If you cannot see Him, look toward the place where you think He is. Remind Him that He is the Author of faith, and that it is His gift. Claim it from Him, and reckon that in answer to your appeal He does confer this priceless boon. You may not feel faith, but you will find yourself unconsciously thinking of Christ, counting on Christ, going out toward Christ; and that engagement of the soul with Christ is faith.

Be careful of the tender plant that has thus been planted within you. Give it plenty of sunshine. Live outside yourself in the consideration of what Christ is. Feed faith on her native food of promise, and let her breathe her native air on the hills of communion. Treat all suggestions of doubt as you would questions as to the fidelity of your dearest friend. Avoid the cold blast that sets in from skeptical books and talk. Be sure to live up to your highest conceptions of duty toward God and man. Your faith will be in exact proportion to your obedience. Inability to trust almost always denotes some failure to obey. If faith is faltering, ask yourself whether you have not dropped the thread of obedience, and go back to the place where you lost it. Christian could not face the lions till he had sorrowfully retraced his steps to the arbor where he had slept and recovered his roll.

Faith is pre-eminently the receptive faculty. It not only reckons that God gives, but it stretches out its hand to take. "As many as *received* him, to them gave he power to become the sons of God, even to them that *believe* on his name" (John 1:12). We receive the at-one-ment from the Lord who died, and we receive the abundance of God's grace from the Lord who ever lives, so that we will reign when the heavens and earth have fled away and there is no more sea to divide us from our beloved (Revelation 21:1). The beautiful garments are prepared, and faith arrays herself in them. The armor hangs on the wall, so faith girds herself in it. The water of life gushes at her feet, but faith catches it up, as did Gideon's three hundred men. Faith thus deals definitely with God. She does not simply see His gifts as the passerby sees the jewel in the shop window, but she knows that all the regalia of God's kingdom are hers, and she takes them as she will. She hears the voice of her Father saying: "You are ever with me, and all that I have is yours."

It was not enough that God should give the land of Canaan by promise and covenant to the chosen race. They had to go in to possess it, to put their foot down on its soil, to till its acres, and to live in its rich products. So it must be with the believer. He is first united with Jesus by a living faith, which *rests* in Him as Savior, Friend, and King; then he reckons that the Son of God is well able to make him His joint-heir of all His boundless wealth; and, lastly, he learns the art of receiving and using the plenteous heritage, and year by year he presses the fences of his possession farther back, taking in more and more of that vast extent of territory that has been assigned to him in Jesus.

Oh! Settler on the boundless continent of God's fullness in Jesus, get up into the high mountain. Look northward, southward, eastward, and westward, over the lengths, and breadths, and depths, and heights of the love of God. It is all yours from the river of Time that rises at your foot to the utmost sea of Eternity. Be not slack to go up and possess the land and to inherit all that God has freely bestowed on you in the Son of His love.

Feeling

Our feelings are very deceptive, because they are so easily wrought on from without. They are affected by the state of our health, changes in the weather, the society or absence of those who love us. When the air is light, and the sun shines, and we have slept well, we are more likely to feel disposed toward God than when the dripping November fog drenches the woodlands. The Father who made us and knows our frame understands this; so much so that when Elijah, after the strain of Carmel, his swift flight, and his disappointment at Jezebel's continued obduracy, threw himself beneath the juniper tree and asked for a swift death, God sent him sleep for his exhausted nervous system and food for his hunger.

As a rule, faith bears fruit in feeling. "Being justified by faith, we have peace with God . . . and [we] rejoice in hope of the glory of God" (Romans 5:1–2). "Believing, ye rejoice with joy unspeakable and full of glory" (1 Peter 1:8). When the prodigal returned, the father bade his servants slay the fatted calf, saying: "Let us eat, and be merry." There is relief from a heavy burden of sin, the ecstasy of pardon, the light of the Father's face, the sense of rightness, the calm outlook on the future. When the King comes to His own, the bells ring out their peals on the waiting air, as though intoxicated with delight!

Happy and blessed feeling is the effect of the Spirit's work on the soul. "The fruit of the Spirit is love, joy, peace . . ." He is the earnest of our inheritance, and though in our childhood we cannot expect to enter into the fullness of our heritage, we are privileged to enjoy its first-fruits. There are foretastes of the river of His pleasures and stray notes from the full chorus of bliss. When the Holy Spirit reveals the Bridegroom, the loving heart is glad, even though the nuptials are not yet celebrated.

But the lack of feeling does not always indicate we are wrong. There may be causes, as we have seen, that account for our depression. It may be that Christ would teach us to distinguish between love and the emotion of love, between joy and the rapture of joy, between peace and the sense of peace. Or perhaps He may desire to ascertain whether we cling to Him for Himself or for His gifts.

Children greet their father from the window as he turns the corner and comes down the street. He hears the rush of their feet along the hall as he inserts his key in the door. But one day he begins to question whether they greet him for the love they bear him or for the gifts with which he never forgets to fill his pockets. One day, therefore, he gives them due notice that there will be no gifts when he returns at night. Their faces fall, but when the hour of return arrives, they are at the window as usual, and there is the same tramping of little feet to the door. "Ah," he says, "my children love me for myself," and he is glad.

Our Father sometimes cuts off the supply of joy and allows us to hunger that He may know what is in our hearts and whether we love Him for Himself. If we still cling to Him as Job did, He is glad and restores comforts to His mourners with both hands.

Seek feeling, and you will miss it; be content to live without it, and you will have all you require. If you are always noticing your heartbeats, you will bring on heart disease. If you are always muffling against cold, you will become very subject to chills. If you are perpetually thinking about your health, you will induce disease. If you are always consulting your feelings, you will live in a dry and thirsty land, where no water is. He that saves his soul shall lose it.

Be indifferent to emotion. If it is there, be thankful; if it is absent, go on doing the will of God, reckoning on Him, speaking well of Him behind His back, and, above all, giving no signs of what you are suffering, lest you be a stumbling block to others. Then joy will overtake you as a flood. He will make you sit at His table and will gird Himself to come forth and serve you.

Cautions

There are five concluding cautions for the culture of the devout life, attention to which will generally result in holy joy and peace.

1. *We must be still before God.* The life around us, in this age, is preeminently one of rush and effort. It is the age of the express train and telegraph. Years are crowded into months, and weeks into days. This feverish haste threatens the religious life. The stream has already entered our churches and stirred their quiet pools. Meetings crowd on meetings. The same energetic souls are found at them all and engaged in many good works beside. But we must beware that we do not substitute the active for the contemplative, the valley for the mountaintop. Neither can with safety be divorced from the other. The sheep must go in and out. The blood

must come back to the heart to be recharged and fitted to be impelled again to the extremities.

We must make time to be alone with God. The closet and the shut door are indispensable. We must lose the glare of the sunny piazza that we may see the calm angel figures bending above the altar. We must escape the din of the world to become accustomed to the accents of the still, small voice. Like David, we must sit before the Lord. Happy are they who have an observatory in their heart-house to which they can often retire beneath the great arch of Eternity, turning their telescope to the mighty constellations that turn beyond life's fever and reaching regions where the breath of human applause or censure cannot follow!

It is only in such moments that the best spiritual gifts will loom in our vision or we shall have grace to receive them. It is impossible to rush into God's presence, catch up anything we fancy, and run off with it. To attempt this will end in mere delusion and disappointment. Nature will not unveil her rarest beauty to the chance tourist. Pictures that are the result of a life of work do not disclose their secret loveliness to the one who saunters down a gallery. No charter can be read at a glance. And God's best cannot be ours apart from patient waiting in His Holy Presence. The superficial may be put off with a parable or a pretty story, but it is not given to such to know the mysteries of the kingdom of heaven.

2. *We must be possessed by an eager desire.* There is a difference between wishing for a thing and willing it. In a single hour we may wish for a hundred differing objects, and forget them. But how different from this is the fixed determination, the settled purpose of the *will!*

The lad catches sight of some equipment for his sport; the student, of a precious book; the lover, of a rare and jeweled ornament that he covets for the one he loves. In each case the will is wrought upon till it resolves to acquire at any cost. Then privation and self-sacrifice and delay are cheerfully encountered. Nothing can extinguish or slacken the determination that follows hard after its quest. So with us. We must hunger and thirst; we must be possessed by strong and passionate desire; we must be resolved even to use violence to take the kingdom of heaven. The expressions of Scripture are all so intense—the deer pants for the water brooks; Jacob will not let the angel go; the widow troubles the unjust judge day and night. We too may have this strong desire if we will let the Spirit of God produce it within our hearts. But the merchant must be bent on seeking and finding the goodly pearl. We must strive to enter the strait gate. We must agonize (to use the apostle's word) as the athlete for the crown.

3. *We must have a promise in our hand.* This is

the true method of dealing with God. Search the Bible for some holy word that exactly fits your case. It will not be hard to find one, since Scripture abounds with personal incidents, culled from every conceivable variety of life. Then, when it has been discovered, and perhaps borne in on you by the divine Spirit, take it with you into the presence of God or place your finger upon it as you pass into the presence-chamber with hushed and reverent step. The promises are our inventory of possession, and our need should make us look for and claim the blessing intended to meet it.

5

BURDENS, AND WHAT
TO DO WITH THEM

Do you keep the Sabbath? Not the literal seventh-day rest, but the inner rest of which that day was the blessed type. The pause in the outward business of life was but a parable of that inner hush, which is not for one day but for all days; not for one race but for all men; not for the hereafter only but for now. The Sabbath-keeping that awaits the people of God, undiminished in a single atom by the storms that have swept around it, is for all faithful souls, who may take it when they will and carry it with them.

> Through dusky land and wrangling mart,
> Plying their daily task with busier feet,
> Because their secret souls a holy strain repeat.

This is a strain borrowed from the eternal chords and harmonies of the life and being of God.

The secret of Sabbath-keeping is in the absence of burden-bearing. "Thus saith the Lord; Take heed to yourselves, and bear no burden on the sabbath day, nor bring it in by the gates of Jerusalem; Neither carry forth a burden out of your houses on the sabbath day" (Jeremiah 17:21–22). And in the words that follow, the continual presence of a king is made to hinge on obedience about burdens. Nehemiah was so urgent in this matter that he set his servants at the city gates, as they crowned the gray summit of Zion, "that there should no burden be brought in on the sabbath day" (Nehemiah 13:19).

And what was true in those bygone days is true always. There can be no true Sabbath-keeping when burdens are freely brought into the precincts of the soul. As well try to sleep when a party of high-spirited, healthy children are tearing up and down the house and playing hide-and-seek in all the rooms. Care will break the rest of the soul as much as sin does. And there is no hope that we should know the peace that passes all understanding till we have learned the art of shutting the door against the long train of burden-carrying thoughts that are always coming up the hill from the world beneath to fill our spirit with the ring of their feet and the clamor of their cries.

We need not stay to describe the results that burden-bearing brings to the heavy-laden. They are evident in the careworn look, the weary eye, the heavy step. But deeper than these, there is no power in prayer, no joy in God, no lying down in green pastures, no walking beside the waters of rest. As snowflakes in the arctic or sand grains in the tropics will build a rampart before some lowly dwelling sufficient to exclude the light, so will worries, each infinitesimal in itself, shut out the blessed light of God from the soul and make midnight where God meant midday.

Burden-bearing sadly dishonors God. As men of the world look upon the faces of those who profess to be God's children and see them dark with the same shadows as are flung across their own, they may well wonder what sort of a Father He is. Whatever be a man's profession, we cannot help judging him by the faces of his children. And if God be judged by the unconscious report made of Him by some of His children, the hardest things ever said against Him by His foes are not far from the truth.

Under such circumstances the unbeliever may fitly argue, "Either there is no God, or He is powerless to help, or He does not really love, or He is careless of the needs of His children. Of what good will religion be to me?"

We are either libel or Bible; harbor lights or warning signals; magnetic or repellent; and which one we are very much depends on how we treat our burdens.

Of course there is a *difference between care and pain;* between bearing the self-made burden of our anxieties and suffering according to the will of God. We must not make light of sufferings sent by our Father to teach lessons that could only be learned in the school in which our Lord and Savior has sat before us to learn obedience. The chastened spirit must go softly and withdraw itself to suffer. But accepting the sufferings sent from God is very different from burden-bearing. There will be no doubt as to the Father's care, no worry about the issues, no foreboding as to the long future, which to the eye of faith gleams like the horizon-rim of the sea on which the sun is shining in splendor, though the dark clouds brood immediately overhead.

Before we are thoroughly awake in the morning we sometimes become conscious of a feeling of depression, as if all were not right; and a voice seems to tell a long tale of burdens to be carried and difficulties to be met as the hours pass by.

"Ah!" says the voice, "a miserable day will this be."

"How so?" we inquire, fearfully.

"Remember there is that creditor to meet, that skein to disentangle, that irritation to soothe, those violent tempers to confront. It is no use praying. Better linger where you are, and then drag through the day as you can. You are like a martyr being led to his death."

And too often we have yielded to the suggestion and have dragged ourselves wearily through the hours, doing our daily tasks with hands engaged and strength spent by the burdens that we have assumed. God is pledged to give strength for all duties that He sets, but not for the burdens that we elect to take on as well.

The one cure for burden-bearing is to cast all burdens on the Lord. The margin of the Revised Version of Psalm 55:22 reads thus: "Cast that He hath given thee upon the Lord." Whatever burden the Lord has given you, give it back to Him. Treat the burden of care as once you did the burden of sin; kneel down and deliberately hand it over to Jesus. Say to Him, "Lord, I entrust to You this, and this, and this. I cannot carry them; they are crushing me, but I definitely commit them all to You to manage, and adjust, and arrange. You have taken my sins. Take my sorrows, and in exchange give me Your peace, Your rest." As George Herbert says, "We must put them all into Christ's bag."

Will not our Lord Jesus be at least as true and faithful as the best earthly friend we have ever known? And have there not been times in all our lives when we have been too weary or helpless to help ourselves and have thankfully handed some wearing anxiety to a good, strong man, sure that when once it was entrusted to him, he would not rest until he had finished it to his satisfaction? Surely He who loved us enough to die for us may be trusted to arrange all the smaller matters of our daily lives!

Of course there are one or two *conditions* that we must fulfill before we shall be able to hand over our burdens to the Lord Jesus and leave them with Him in perfect confidence. We must have cast our sins on Him before we can cast our cares. We must be at peace with God through the work of our Savior before we can have the peace of God through faith in His gracious interposition on our behalf. We must also be living on God's plan, tarrying under the cloud, obeying His laws and executing His plans so far as we know them. We must also feed faith with promise, for this food is essential to make it thrive. And when we have done all this we shall not find it so difficult

> To kneel, and cast our load,
> E'en while we pray upon our God.
> Then rise with lightened cheer.

Hand Over to Christ the Burden of How to Grow in Grace

This is a very great burden to some earnest people. They go from convention to convention, from one speaker to another, notebook in hand, so eager to get the blessing (as they term it) and often thinking more of the rapture of the gift than of the person of the Giver. And because they hear of others having experiences that they know not, they carry heavy burdens of disappointment and self-reproach.

Equally well might a child in kindergarten fret because he is not entered in the higher classes of the school. But why should he worry about his future progress? His one business is to acquire the lessons set him by his teacher. When those are learned it will be for the teacher to teach his pupil more and to advance him to positions where quicker progress may be made. And it is for us to learn the lessons that the Lord Jesus sets before us day by day, leaving Him to lead us into the fuller knowledge and love of God.

Thomas was one of the dull pupils in our Master's school. He could not see what was clear to all beside. But instead of chiding him and leaving him to grope in the dark, the Master paid him a special visit and made the glad fact of His resurrection so simple that the doubter was able to rejoice with the rest. Don't worry about your dullness; it will only mean that the dear Master will give you longer and more personal attention. Mothers give most pains to the sickly, weak, and slow among their children.

Hand Over to Christ the Burden of Maintaining a Christian Profession

Many are kept from identifying themselves openly with the Lord's people by a secret feeling that they will never be able to hold out. They carry with them a nervous dread of bringing disgrace on their Christian profession and trailing Christ's colors in the dust. Almost unconsciously, they repeat the words of David, "I

shall now perish one day by the hand of Saul"
(1 Samuel 27:1).

Anxiety about so sacred a matter as this will
hide the face of Christ, as the impalpable vapor-
wreaths hide the majestic, snow-capped peaks.
And it is quite needless. He who saved can
uphold. As is His heart of love, so is His arm of
might. He is able to keep us from stumbling
and present us faultless before the presence of
His glory. But we shall never know the sufficiency of that keeping while we cling to the boat
or even keep one hand upon its side. Only when
we have stepped right out onto the water, relying utterly on the Master's power, shall we know
how blessedly and certainly He keeps what is
committed to Him against that day.

We must not carry even the burden of daily
abiding in Him. Let us rather trust Him to
keep us trusting and abiding in Himself. He
will not fail us if we do, and He will answer our
faith by giving us an appetite for those exercis-
es of prayer, Bible study, and communion that
are the secrets of unbroken fellowship.

Hand Over to Christ the Burden of Christian Work

How to maintain our congregations; how
to hold our ground amid the competition of
neighboring workers; how to sustain the vigor
and efficiency of our machinery; how to adjust
the differences arising between fellow and sub-

ordinate workers; how to find material enough for sermons and addresses—beneath the pressure of burdens like these how many workers break down! They could bear the work, but not the worry.

And yet the responsibility of the work is not ours but our Master's. He is bearing this world in His arms, as a mother her sick child. He is ministering to the infinite need of man. He is carrying on His great redemptive scheme for the glory of His Father. All He wants of us is a faithful performance of the daily tasks He gives.

Let the sailor lad sleep soundly in his hammock; the captain knows exactly the ship's course. Let the errand boy be content to fetch and carry as he is bidden; the heads of the firm know what they are about and have plenty of resources to meet all their needs. And let the Christian worker guard against bearing burdens that the Lord alone can carry. The Lord would never have sent us to His work without first calculating His ability to carry us through.

Hand Over to Christ the Burden of the Ebb and Flow of Feeling

Our feelings are as changeable as April weather. They are affected by an infinite number of subtle causes—our physical health, the state of the atmosphere, overweariness, want of sleep—as well as by those that are spiritual and inward. No stringed instrument is more liable to be affected by minute changes than we are. And we are apt to take it sorely to heart when we see the tide of emotion running out fast.

At such times we should question ourselves, to see whether our lack of feeling is due to conscious sin or worrying; and, if not, we may hand over all further anxiety in the matter to Him who knows our frame and remembers that we are dust. As we pass down the dark staircase, let us hold fast to the handrail of His will, willing to do His will, though in the dark. "I am as much Your own, equally devoted to You now in the depths of my soul, as when I felt happiest in Your love."

Hand Over to Christ All Other Burdens

Servants with their frequent changes; employers with unreasonable demands; unkind gossip and slanderous tales that are being circulated about you; the perplexities and adversities of business; the difficulties of making two ends meet; the question of changing your residence, or situation, and obtaining another; children with the ailments of childhood and the waywardness of youth; provision for sickness and old age. There are some whose businesses are peculiarly trying and liable to cause anxious thought, others whose horizon is always bounded by the gaunt specters of poverty.

Any one of these will break our rest, as one barking dog may break our slumber in the stillest night, and as one grain of dust in the eye will render it incapable of enjoying the fairest prospect.

There is nothing for us, then, but to roll our burden, and indeed, ourselves, on God (Psalm 55:22). When a little boy, trying to help his father move some books, fell on the stairs beneath the weight of a heavy volume, the father ran to his aid and caught up boy and burden both, and bore them in his arms to his own room. And will our Father do less? He must love us infinitely and be ever at hand. "He careth for you" (1 Peter 5:7).

It is a good way in dealing with God, and if you are not quite sure of His will, to say that you will stay where you are, or go on doing what you have been doing, until He makes quite clear what He wants and empowers you to do it. Roll the responsibility of your way on God (Proverbs 16:3), and expect that He will make known to you any alteration that He desires in a way so unmistakable that, though you are dull and stupid, you may not mistake it.

Don't worry about dress, or ornaments, or doubtful things. Satan loves to turn the soul's attention from Christ to itself. It is as if a girl should spend an hour in her room wondering in what dress to meet her lover, who is waiting impatiently below. Let her go to him, and if she desires it, he will soon enough tell her clearly what he prefers. Get into the presence of Jesus, and you will not be left to hazy questioning and doubtful disputations, but will be told clearly and unmistakably His will, and always definitely about one point at a time.

Archbishop Leighton sweetly says: "When thou art either to do or suffer anything, when thou art about any purpose of business, go, tell God about it, and acquaint Him with it—yea, burden Him with it—and thou hast done for matter of caring. No more care, but sweet, quiet diligence in thy duty, and dependence on Him for the carriage of thy matters. Roll over on God, make one bundle of all: roll thy cares, and thyself with them, as one burden, all on thy God."

And so, when no burdens are brought into the soul, but are handed immediately over to the blessed Lord, the peace of God will fill the inner temple. And though outside there may be the strife of tongues, and the chafe of this restless world, like the troubled sea when it cannot rest, and the pressure of many engagements, yet these things shall expand themselves on the battlements of the life which is the environing presence of God; while, within, the soul keeps an unbroken Sabbath, like the unruffled ocean depths, which are not stirred by the hurricanes that churn the surface into foam and fury. "The peace of God, which passeth all understanding, shall keep your hearts and minds through Christ Jesus" (Philippians 4:7).

6

HOW TO BEAR SORROW

You are passing through a time of deep sorrow. The love on which you were trusting has suddenly failed you and dried up like a brook in the desert that is now a dwindling stream, then shallow pools, and at last drought. You are always listening for footsteps that do not come, waiting for a word that is not spoken, pining for a reply that tarries overdue.

Perhaps the savings of your life have suddenly disappeared. Instead of helping others, you must be helped; or you must leave the warm nest where you have been sheltered from life's storms to go alone into an unfriendly world; or you are suddenly called to assume the burden of some other life, taking no rest for yourself till you have steered it through dark and difficult seas into the haven. Your health, sight, or nervous energy is failing; you carry in yourself the sentence of death; and the anguish of anticipating the future is almost unbearable. In other cases there is the sense of recent loss through death, like the gap in the forest where the woodsman has lately been felling trees.

At such times life seems almost insupportable. Will every day be as long as this? Will the slow-moving hours ever again quicken their pace? Will life ever array itself in another garb than the torn autumn remnants of past summer glory? "Hath God forgotten to be gracious? hath he in anger shut up his tender mercies?" (Psalm 77:9).

This road has been trodden by myriads. When you think of the desolating wars that have swept through every country and devastated every land; of the expeditions of the Nimrods, the Nebuchadnezzars, the Timurs, the Napoleons of history; of the merciless slave trade, and of all the tyranny, the oppression, the wrong that the weak and defenseless have suffered at the hands of their fellows; of the unutterable sorrows of women and children—surely you must see that by far the larger number of our race have passed through the same bitter griefs as those that rend your heart.

Jesus Christ Himself trod this difficult path, leaving traces of His blood on its flints; and apostles, prophets, confessors, and martyrs have passed by the same way. It is comforting to know that others have traversed the same dark valley and that the great multitudes that stand before the Lamb, wearing palms of victory, came out of great tribulation. Where they were, we are; and, by God's grace, where they are, we shall be.

Do Not Talk About Punishment

You may talk of chastisement or correction, for our Father deals with us as with sons; or you may speak of reaping the results of mistakes and sins dropped as seeds into life's furrows in former years; or you may have to bear the consequences of the sins and mistakes of others; but do not speak of punishment. Surely all the guilt and penalty of sin were laid on Jesus, and He put them away forever. His were the stripes and the chastisement of our peace. If God punishes us for our sins, it would seem that the sufferings of Christ were incomplete; and if He once began to punish us, life would be too short for the infliction of all that we deserve. Besides, how could we explain the anomalies of life, and the heavy sufferings of the saints as compared with the carefree life of the ungodly? Surely, if our sufferings were penal, there would be a reversal of these lots.

Sorrow is a refiner's crucible. It may be caused by the neglect or cruelty of another, by circumstances over which the sufferer has no control, or as the direct result of some dark hour in the long past; but inasmuch as God has permitted it to come, it must be accepted as His appointment and considered as the furnace by which He is searching, testing, probing, and purifying the soul. Suffering searches us as fire does metal. We think we are fully for God until we are exposed to the cleansing fire of pain. Then we discover, as Job did, how much dross there is in us, and how little real patience, submission, and faith. Nothing so detaches us from the things of this world, the life of sense, the snare of earthly affections. There is probably no other way by which the power of the self life can be arrested, that the life of Jesus may be manifested in our mortal flesh.

But God always keeps the discipline of sorrow in His own hands. Our Lord said, "My Father is the husbandman." His hand holds the pruning knife. His eye watches the crucible. His gentle touch is on the pulse while the operation is in progress. He will not allow even the devil to have his own way with us. As in the case of Job, so always. The moments are carefully allotted. The severity of the test is exactly determined by the reserves of grace and strength that are lying unrecognized within, but will be sought for and used beneath the severe pressure of pain. He holds the winds in His fist and the waters in the hollow of His hand. He dares not risk the loss of that which has cost Him the blood of His Son. "God is faithful, who will not suffer you to be [tried] above that ye are able" (1 Corinthians 10:13).

In sorrow the Comforter is near. "Very present in time of trouble." He *sits* by the crucible, as a Refiner of silver, regulating the heat, marking every change, waiting patiently for the scum to float away and His own face to be mirrored in clear, translucent metal. No earthly friend may tread the winepress with you, but the Savior is there, His garments stained with the blood of the grapes of your sorrow. Dare to repeat it often, though you do not feel it, and though Satan insists that God has left you, *"You are with me."* Mention His name again and again, "Jesus, *Jesus,* You are with me." So you will become conscious that He is there.

When friends come to console you, they talk of time's healing touch, as though the best balm for sorrow were to forget; or in their well-meant kindness, they suggest travel, diversion, or amusement, and they show their inability to appreciate the black night that hangs over your soul. So you turn from them sick at heart and prepared to say, as Job, "Miserable comforters are ye all." But all the while Jesus is nearer than they are, understanding how they wear you, knowing each throb of pain, touched by fellow-feeling, silent in a love too full to speak, waiting to comfort from hour to hour as a mother comforts her weary and suffering baby.

Be sure to study the art of this divine comfort, that you may be able to comfort those who are in any affliction with the comfort with which you yourself have been comforted by God (2 Corinthians 1:4). There can be no doubt that some trials are permitted to come to us, as to our Lord, for no other reason than that by means of them we should become able to give sympathy and succor to others. And we should watch with all care each symptom of the pain and each prescription of the Great Physician, since in all probability at some future time we shall be called to minister to those passing through similar experiences. Thus we learn by the things that we suffer and, being made perfect, become authors of priceless and eternal help to souls in agony.

Do Not Shut Yourself Up with Your Sorrow

A friend, in the first anguish of bereavement, wrote saying that he must give up the Christian ministries in which he had delighted; and I replied immediately, urging him not to do so, because there is no solace for heart-pain like ministry. The temptation of great suffering is toward isolation, withdrawal from the life of men, sitting alone, and keeping silence. Do not yield to it. Break through the icy chains of reserve, if they have already gathered. Arise, anoint your head and wash your face; go forth to your duty, with willing though chastened steps.

Selfishness of every kind, in its activities or its introspection, is a hurtful thing, and shuts out the help and love of God. Sorrow is apt to be selfish. The soul, occupied with its own griefs, and refusing to be comforted, becomes presently a Dead Sea, full of brine and salt, over which the birds do not fly, and beside which no green thing grows. And thus we miss the very lesson that God would teach us. His constant war is against the self-life, and every pain He inflicts is to lessen its hold upon us. But we may thwart His purpose and extract poison from His gifts, as men get opium and alcohol from innocent plants.

A Hindu woman, a beautiful Eastern legend tells us, lost her only child. Wild with grief, she implored a prophet to give back her little one to her love. He looked at her tenderly for a long while and said:

"Go, my daughter, bring me a handful of rice from a house into which Death has never entered, and I will do as you desire."

The woman at once began her search. She went from dwelling to dwelling, and had no difficulty in obtaining rice; but when the people had granted it, she inquired: "Are you all here around the hearth—father, mother, children—none missing?"

The people invariably shook their heads, with sighs and looks of sadness. As far and wide as she wandered, there was always some vacant seat by the hearth. And gradually, as she passed on, the legend says, the waves of her grief subsided before the spectacle of sorrow everywhere; and her heart ceased to be occupied with its own individual pang as it flowed out in strong yearnings of sympathy with the universal suffering. Tears of anguish softened into tears of pity; passion melted away in compassion; she forgot herself in the general interest; and she found redemption in redeeming.

Do Not Chide Yourself for Feeling Strongly

Tears are natural. Jesus wept. A thunderstorm without rain is fraught with peril; the pattering raindrops cool the air and relieve the overcharged atmosphere. The swollen brooks indicate that the snow is melting on the hills and spring is near. "Daughters of Jerusalem," said our Lord, "weep for yourselves, and for your children" (Luke 23:28).

To bear sorrow with dry eyes and stolid heart may befit a Stoic, but not a Christian. We have no need to rebuke fond nature crying for is mate, its lost joy, the touch of the vanished hand, the sound of the voice that is still, provided only that the will is surrendered. This is the one consideration for those who suffer—*Is the will right?* If it isn't, God Himself cannot comfort. If it is, then the path will inevitably lead from the valley of the shadow of death to the banqueting table and the overflowing cup.

Many say: "I cannot feel surrendered. It is bad enough to have my grief to bear, but I have this added trouble, that I cannot *feel* surrendered."

My invariable reply is: "You probably never can feel surrender, but you can *will* it."

The Lord Jesus, in the Garden of Gethsemane, has shown us how to suffer. He chose

His Father's will. Though Judas, prompted by Satan, was the instrument for mixing the cup and placing it to the Savior's lips, He looked right beyond him to the Father, who permitted him to work his cruel way, and said: "The cup which my Father hath given me, shall I not drink it?" And He said repeatedly, "If this cup may not pass away from me, except I drink it, thy will be done." He gave up His own way and will, saying, "I will Thy will, O My Father. Thy will, and not Mine, be done."

Let all sufferers who read these lines go apart and dare to say the same words: "Your will, and not mine. Your will be done in the earth of my life, as in the heaven of Your purpose. I choose Your will." Say this thoughtfully and deliberately, not because you can *feel* it, but because you *will* it; not because the way of the cross is pleasant, but because it must be right. Say it repeatedly, whenever the surge of pain sweeps through you, whenever the wound begins to bleed afresh. "Not my will, but Yours be done." *Dare to say Yes to God.* "Even so, Father, for so it seems good in Your sight."

And so you will be led to feel that all is right and well. A great calm will settle down on your heart, a peace that passes understanding, a sense of rest, which is not inconsistent with suffering, but walks in the midst of it as the three young men in the fiery furnace, to whom the burning coals must have been like the dewy grass of a forest glade.

"The doctor told us my little child was dying. I felt like a stone. But *in a moment* I seemed to give up my hold on her. She appeared no longer mine, but God's."

Be Sure to Learn God's Lessons

Each sorrow carries at its heart a germ of holy truth, which if you get and sow in the soil of your heart will bear harvests of fruit, as seedcorns from mummy-cases bear fruit in modern soil. God has a meaning in each blow of His chisel, each incision of His knife. He knows the way that He takes. But His object is not always clear to us.

In suffering and sorrow God touches the minor chords, develops the passive virtues, and opens to view the treasures of darkness, the constellations of promise, the rainbow of hope, the silver light of the covenant. What is character without sympathy, submission, patience, trust, and hope that grips the unseen as an anchor? But these graces are only possible through sorrow. Sorrow is a garden, the trees of which are laden with the peaceable fruits of righteousness; do not leave it without bringing them with you. Sorrow is a mine, the walls of which glisten with precious stones; be sure and do not retrace your steps into daylight without some specimens. Sorrow is a school. You are sent to sit on its hard benches and learn from its black-lettered pages lessons that will make you wise forever; do not trifle away your chance of graduating there. Miss Havergal used to talk of "turned lessons."

Count on the afterward. God will not always be causing grief. He traverses the dull brown acres with His plow, seaming the yielding earth that He may be able to cast in the precious grain. Believe that in days of sorrow He is sowing light for the righteous and gladness for the upright in heart. Look forward to the reaping. Anticipate the joy that is set before you and that shall flood your heart with minstrel notes when patience has had her perfect work.

You will live to recognize the wisdom of God's choice for you. You will one day see that the thing you wanted was only second best. You will be surprised to remember that you once nearly broke your heart and spilled the wine of your life for what would never have satisfied you if you had caught it, as the child the butterfly or soap bubble. You will meet again your beloved. You will have again your love. You will become possessed of a depth of character, a breadth of sympathy, a fund of patience, an ability to understand and help others, which, as you lay them at Christ's feet for Him to use, will make you glad that you were afflicted. You will see God's plan and purpose; you will reap His harvest; you will behold His face and be satisfied. Each wound will have its pearl; each car-cass will contain a swarm of bees; each foe will yield its goodly spoil, like Midian did to Gideon.

The way of the cross, rightly borne, is the only way to the everlasting light. Only the path that threads the Garden of Gethsemane and climbs over the hill of Calvary leads to the visions of the Easter morning and the glories of the Ascension mount. If we will not drink of His cup, or be baptized with His baptism, or fill up that which is behind of His sufferings, we cannot expect to share in the joys of His espousals and the ecstasy of His triumph. But if these conditions are fulfilled, we shall not miss one note in the everlasting song, one element in the bliss that is possible to men.

Remember that somehow suffering rightly borne enriches and helps mankind. The death of Hallam was the birthday of Tennyson's beautiful poem "In Memoriam." The cloud of insanity that brooded over Cowper gave us the hymn, "God Moves in a Mysterious Way." Milton's blunders taught him to sing of "Holy light, offspring of heaven's first-born." Rist used to say, "The cross has pressed many songs out of me." And it is probable that none rightly suffer anywhere without contributing something to the allevia-tion of human grief, to the triumph of good over evil, of love over hate, and of light over darkness.

If you believe this, could you not bear to suffer? Is not the chief misery of all suffering its loneliness and perhaps its apparent aimlessness? Then dare to believe that no man dieth to himself. Fall into the ground, bravely and cheerfully, to die. If you refuse this, you will abide alone; but if you yield to it, you will bear fruit that will sweeten the lot and strengthen the lives of others who perhaps will never know your name or stop to thank you for your help.

7

IN THE SECRET OF
HIS PRESENCE

In one sense God is always near us. He is
not an absentee, needing to be brought down
from the heavens or up from the deep. He is
near at hand. His Being pervades all being.
Every world that floats like an island in the
ocean of space is filled with signs of His presence, just as the home of your friend is littered
with many evidences of his residence, by which
you know that he lives there, though you have
not seen his face. Every crocus pushing through
the dark mold; every firefly in the forest; every
bird that springs up from its nest before your
feet; everything that is—*all* are as full of God's
presence as the bush that burned with His fire,
before which Moses bared his feet in acknowl-
edgment that God was there.

But we do not always realize it. We often
pass hours, and days, and weeks. We sometimes
engage in seasons of prayer, we go to and fro
from His house, where the ladder of communication rests; and still He is a shadow, a name, a
tradition, a dream of days gone by.

Oh that I knew where I might find him! that I
might come even to his seat! . . . Behold, I go

forward, but he is not there; and backward, but I cannot perceive him: On the left hand, where he doth work, but I cannot behold him: he hideth himself on the right hand, that I cannot see him. (Job 23:3, 8–9)

How different is this failure to realize the presence of God to the blessed experience of His nearness realized by some!

Brother Lawrence, the simple cook, for more than sixty years never lost the sense of the presence of God, but was as conscious of it while performing the duties of his humble office as when partaking of the Holy Supper.

John Howe, on the blank page of his Bible, made this record in Latin: "This very morning I awoke out of a most ravishing and delightful dream, when a wonderful and copious stream of celestial rays, from the lofty throne of the Divine Majesty, seemed to dart into my open and expanded breast. I have often since reflected on that very signal pledge of special Divine favor, and have with repeated fresh pleasure tasted the delights thereof."

Are not these experiences, so blessed and inspiring, similar to that of the author of the longest, and in some respects, the sublimest Psalm in the Psalter? He had been beating out the golden ore of thought through the successive paragraphs of marvelous power and beauty, when suddenly he seems to have become conscious that He of whom he had been speaking had drawn near, and was bending over him. The sense of the presence of God was borne in upon this inner consciousness. And, lifting up a face on which reverence and ecstasy met and mingled, he cried, "Thou art near, O Lord" (Psalm 119:151).

If only such an experience of the nearness of God were always ours, enfolding us as air or light; if only we could feel, as the great apostle put it on Mars' Hill, that God is not far away, but the element in which we have our being, as sea flowers live in deep, still lagoons: then we should understand what David meant when he spoke about dwelling in the house of the Lord all the days of his life, beholding His beauty, inquiring in His temple, and hiding in the secret of His pavilion (Psalm 27:4–5). Then, too, we should acquire the blessed secret of *peace, purity, and power.*

In the Secret of His Presence
There Is Peace

"In the world ye shall have tribulation," our Master said, but "in me ye might have peace" (John 16:33). It is said that a certain insect has the power of surrounding itself with a film of air, encompassed in which it drops into the midst of muddy, stagnant pools and remains unhurt. And the believer is also conscious that he is enclosed in the invisible film of the divine presence, as a far-traveled letter in the envelope that protects it from hurt and soil.

"They draw nigh that follow after mischief," but You are nearer than the nearest, and I dwell in the inner ring of Your presence. The mountains round about me are filled with the horses and chariots of Your protection. No weapon that is formed against me can prosper, for it can only reach me through You, and, touching You, it will glance harmlessly aside.

To be in God is to be in a well-fitted house when the storm has slipped from its leash; or in a sanctuary, the doors of which shut out the pursuer.

In the Secret of His Presence There Is Purity

The mere vision of snow-capped Alps, seen from afar across Lake Geneva, so elevates and transfigures the rapt and wistful soul as to destroy all evil things that would thrust themselves upon the inner life. The presence of a little child, with his guileless purity, has been known to disarm passion, as a beam of light, falling in a reptile-haunted cave, scatters the snakes.

But what shall not Your presence do for me, if I acquire a perpetual sense of it, and live in its secret place? Surely, in the heart of that fire, black cinder though I be, I shall be kept pure, and glowing, and intense!

In the Secret of His Presence
There Is Power

My cry, day and night, is for power—spiritual power. Not the power of intellect, oratory, or human might. These cannot avail to vanquish the serried ranks of evil.

You say truly that it is not by might nor by power. Yet human souls that touch You become magnetized, charged with a spiritual force that the world can neither gainsay nor resist. Oh! let me touch You! Let me dwell in unbroken contact with You, that out of You successive tides of divine energy may pass into and through my emptied and eager spirit, flowing, but never ebbing, and lifting me into a life of blessed ministry, which shall make deserts blossom like the garden of the Lord.

But how shall we get and keep this sense of God's nearness? Must we go back to Bethel, with its pillar of stone where even Jacob said, "Surely the Lord is in this place" (Genesis 28:16)? Ah, we might have stood beside him, with unanointed eye, and seen no ladder, heard no voice; while the patriarch would discover God in the bare moorlands of our lives, trodden by us without reverence or joy.

Must we travel to the mouth of the cave in whose shadow Elijah stood, thrilled by the music of the still small voice, sweeter by contrast with the thunder and the storm? Alas! we might have stood beside him unconscious of that glorious

Presence; while Elijah, if living now, would discern it in the whisper of the wind, the babbling of babies, the rhythm of heartbeats.

If we had stationed ourselves in our present state beside the apostle Paul when he was caught into the third heaven, we should probably have seen nothing but a tentmaker's shop, or a dingy room in a hired lodging—we in the dark, while he was in transports; while he would discern, were he to live again, angels on our steamships, visions in our temples, doors opening into heaven amid the tempered glories of our more somber skies.

In point of fact, we carry everywhere our circumference of light or dark. God is as much in the world as He was when Enoch walked with Him and Moses communed with Him face-to-face. He is as willing to be a living, bright, glorious Reality to us as to them. But the fault is with us. Our eyes are unanointed because our hearts are not right. The pure in heart still see God, and to those who love Him, and do His commandments, He still manifests Himself as He does not to the world. Let us cease to blame our times; let us blame ourselves. We are degenerate, not they.

What, then, is that temper of soul that most readily perceives the presence and nearness of God? Let us endeavor to learn the blessed secret of abiding ever in the secret of His presence and of being hidden in His pavilion (Psalm 31:20).

Remember, then, at the outset, that neither you nor any of our race can have that glad consciousness of the presence of God except *through Jesus*. None knows the Father but the Son and those to whom the Son reveals Him (Luke 10:22); and none comes to the Father but by Him (John 14:6). Apart from Jesus the presence of God is an object of terror, from which devils wish to hide themselves and sinners weave aprons or hide among the trees to cover themselves. But in Him all barriers are broken down, all veils rent, all clouds dispersed. The weakest believer may live, where Moses sojourned, in the midst of the fire, before whose consuming flames no impurity can stand.

"What part of the Lord's work is most closely connected with this blessed sense of the presence of God?"

It is through the blood of His Cross that sinners are made near. In His death He not only revealed the tender love of God, but He put away our sins and wove for us those garments of stainless beauty, in which we are gladly welcomed into the inner presence-chamber of the King. Remember it is said, "I will commune with thee from above the mercyseat" (Exodus 25:22). And it is when you enter into deepest fellowship with Him in His death, and live most constantly in the spirit of His memorial supper, that you shall realize most deeply His nearness. Now, as at Emmaus, He loves to make Himself known in the breaking of bread.

"And is this all? for I have heard this many times, and still fail to live in the secret place as I would."

Exactly so; and therefore, to do for us what no effort of ours could do, our Lord has received of His Father the promise of the Holy Spirit, that He should bring into our hearts the very presence of God. Understand that since you are Christ's, the blessed Comforter is yours. He is within you as He was within your Lord, and in proportion as you live in the Spirit, and walk in the Spirit, and open your entire nature to Him, you will find yourself becoming His Presence-chamber, irradiated with the light of His glory. And as you realize that He is in you, you will realize that you are ever in Him. Thus the beloved apostle wrote, "Hereby know we that we dwell in him, and he in us, because he hath given us of his Spirit" (1 John 4:13).

"All this I know, and yet I fail to realize this marvelous fact of the indwelling of the Spirit in me; how then can I ever realize my indwelling in Him?"

It is because your life is so hurried. You do not take time enough for meditation and prayer. The Spirit of God within you and the Presence of God without you cannot be discerned while the senses are occupied with pleasure, or the pulse beats quickly, or the brain is filled with the tread of many hurrying thoughts. It is when water stands that it becomes clear and reveals the pebbly beach below. Be still, and know that God is within you and around you. In the hush of the soul the unseen becomes visible, and the eternal real. The eye dazzled by the sun cannot detect the beauties of its pavilion till it has had time to rid itself of the glare. Let no day pass without its season of silent waiting before God.

"Are there any other conditions that I should fulfill, so that I may abide in the secret of His presence?"

Be pure in heart. Every permitted sin encrusts the windows of the soul with thicker layers of grime, obscuring the vision of God. But every victory over impurity and selfishness clears the spiritual vision, and there fall from the eyes, as it had been, scales. In the power of the Holy Spirit deny self, give no quarter to sin, resist the devil, and you shall see God.

The unholy soul could not see God even though it were set down in the midst of heaven. But holy souls see God amid the ordinary commonplaces of earth and find everywhere an open vision. Such could not be nearer God though they stood by the sea of glass. Their only advantage there would be that the veil of their mortal and sinful natures having been rent, the vision would be more direct and perfect.

Keep His commandments. Let there be not one jot or tittle unrecognized and unkept. "He that hath my commandments, and keepeth them, he it is that loveth me: and he that loveth me shall be loved of my Father, and I will love him, and will manifest myself to him" (John 14:21). Moses the faithful servant, was also the prophet, and he spoke with God face to face as a man speaks with his friend.

Continue in the spirit of prayer. Sometimes the vision will tarry to test the earnestness and steadfastness of your desire. At other times it will come as the dawn steals over the sky, and, before you are aware, you will find yourself conscious that He is near. He was even accustomed to glide, unheralded, into the midst of His disciples through unopened doors. "Thy footsteps are not known" (Psalm 77:19).

At such times we may truly say with St. Bernard: "He entered not by the eyes, for His presence was not marked by color; nor by the ears, for there was no sound; nor by the breath, for He mingled not with the air; nor by the touch, for He was impalpable. You ask, then, how I knew that He was present. Because He was a quickening power. As soon as He entered, He awoke my slumbering soul. He moved and pierced my heart, which before was strange, stony, hard and sick, so that my soul could bless the Lord, and all that is within me praised His Holy Name."

Cultivate the habit of speaking aloud to God. Not perhaps always, because our desires are often too sacred or deep to be put into words. But it is well to acquire the habit of speaking to God as to a present friend while sitting in the house or walking by the way. Seek the habit of talking things over with God—letters, your plans, your hopes, your mistakes, your sorrows and sins. Things look very different when brought into the calm light of His presence. One cannot talk long with God aloud without feeling that He is near.

Meditate much upon the Word. This is the garden where the Lord God walks, the temple where He dwells, the presence-chamber where He holds court, and it is found by those who seek Him. It is through the word that we feed upon the Word. And He said, "He that eateth my flesh, and drinketh my blood, dwelleth in me, and I in him" (John 6:56).

Be diligent in Christian work. The place of prayer is indeed the place of His manifested presence, but that presence would fade from it were we to linger there after the bell of duty had rung for us below. We shall ever meet it as we go about our necessary work: "Thou meetest him that . . . worketh righteousness" (Isaiah 64:5). As we go forth to our daily tasks the angel of His presence comes to greet us and turns to go at our side. "Go ye," said the Master; "Lo, I am with you alway" (Matthew 28:19–20). Not only in temple courts, or in sequestered glens, or in sickrooms, but in the round of daily duty, in the common places of life, on the dead levels of existence, we may be ever in the secret of His presence, and shall be able to say with Elijah before Ahab, and with Gabriel to Zacharias, "I stand in the presence of God" (see 1 Kings 17:1; Luke 1:19).

Cultivate the habit of recognizing the presence of God. "Blessed is the man whom thou choosest, and causest to approach unto thee, that he may dwell in thy courts" (Psalm 65:4). There is no life like this. To feel that God is with us; that He never leads us through a place too narrow for Him to pass as well; that we can never be lonely again, never for a single moment; that we are beset by Him behind and before, and covered by His hand; that He could not be nearer to us, even if we were in heaven itself. To have Him as Friend, and Referee, and Counselor, and Guide. To realize that there is never to be a Jericho in our lives without the presence of the Captain of the Lord's host, with those invisible but mighty legions, before whose charge all walls must fall down. What wonder that saints of old waxed valiant in fight as they heard Him say, "I will be with thee: I will not fail thee, nor forsake thee" (Joshua 1:5).

Begone fear and sorrow and dread of the dark valley! "Thou shalt hide [me] in the secret of thy presence from the pride of man: thou shalt keep [me] secretly in a pavilion from the strife of tongues" (Psalm 31:20).

8

THE FULLNESS OF THE SPIRIT

"Be filled with the Spirit." Ephesians 5:18

Nothing can compensate the church, or the individual Christian, for the lack of the Holy Spirit. What the full stream is to the mill wheel, that the Holy Spirit is to the church. What the principle of life is to the body, that the Holy Spirit is to the individual. We shall stand powerless and abashed in the presence of our difficulties and our foes until we learn what He can be, as a mighty tide of love and power in the hearts of His saints.

Among the readers of these lines there may be many who are suffering from different forms of spiritual weakness, all of which are directly attributable to the lack of the Holy Spirit. Not that they are completely destitute of Him, for if they were, they would not be Christians at all; but that, being within them, He is present only as an attenuated thread, a silver streak, a shallow brook. Why should we be content with this? The fullness of the Day of Pentecost, the endowment of power, the baptism of fire, are all within our reach. Let us be inspired with a holy ambition to get all that our God is willing to bestow.

It is not difficult to show this contrast by analogies drawn from the Word of God. May we not reverently say that the ministry of our blessed Lord Himself owed much of its marvelous power to the moment when, although filled with the Holy Spirit from His birth, He was anointed afresh at the water of baptism? With marked emphasis it was said that He was filled with the Spirit (Luke 4:1), returned in the power of the Spirit into Galilee (v. 14), and stood up in the synagogue of His native town, claiming the ancient prophecy, and declaring that the Spirit of God was upon Him (v. 18). His wondrous words and works are directly traced to the marvelous operation of the Holy Spirit upon His human life (Acts 10:38).

Do you lack *assurance?* Sometimes you have felt happy and content. But these happy hours have fled, and your rest is broken as the surface of the mountain lake is overcast and ruffled by the gathering storm. You need a basis of settled peace, and it is only to be found, first, in a clear apprehension of what Jesus has done for you; secondly, in the sealing of the Holy Spirit. It is His sacred office to witness with our spirit that we are the children of God. He is the Spirit of adoption, whereby we cry, "Abba, Father!"

Do you lack *victory over sin?* This is not to be wondered at, if you neglect the Holy Spirit. He

is the blessed antidote to the risings and dominion of the flesh. He wars against the flesh, so
that we may not fulfill its lusts. When He fills
the heart with His glorious fullness, the suggestions of temptation are instantly quenched, as
sparks in the ocean wave. Sin can no more
stand against the presence of the Holy Spirit
than darkness can resist the gentle, all-pervasive
beams of morning light.

If, however, He is grieved, resisted, or
quenched, so that His power and presence are
restrained, there is no deliverance for the spirit, however bitter its remorse or eager its resort
to fastings, mortification, and regrets. The law
of the spirit of life, which is in Christ Jesus, can
alone make us free from the law of sin and
death. But it can, and it will, only if we yield
ourselves to its operation.

Do you lack the *fruits of holiness*? Some whom
we know are so evidently filled with the fruits of
righteousness, which are the praise of God,
that we are instinctively drawn to them. Their
faces are bright with the presence of the Lord
although they drink of the cup of His sorrows.
Their spirit is tender, their disposition sweet
and unselfish, and their childlike humility
flings the halo of indescribable beauty over
their whole behavior. We lack these graces.
There is little in us to attract men to Christ,
much to repel. Our boughs are naked and
bare, as if locusts had stripped them. And the

reason is evident. We have not let the Holy Spirit have His way with our inner life. Had the sap of His presence been mightily within us, we should have been laden with luscious fruit; it would have been impossible to be otherwise.

Do you lack *power for service?* You have no burning thirst for the salvation of others. You are not on fire for souls. You have never been in agony over the alienation of men from God. And when you speak, there is no power in what you say. The demons laugh at your attempts to exorcise them. The sleeper turns for a moment uneasily, but soon falls into more profound slumber than ever. The home, the class, and the congregation yield no results. No hand-picked fruit fills your basket. No shoal of fish breaks your nets. No recruits accept your call to arms. And you cannot expect it to be otherwise till you obtain the power that our Lord promised when He said: "Ye shall receive power, after that the Holy Ghost is come upon you" (Acts 1:8). It was when the early Christians were filled with the Holy Spirit that they spoke the Word of God with boldness and gave witness with great power to the resurrection of the Lord Jesus.

These and many other deficiencies would be met, if only we were filled with the Holy Spirit. There would be a joy, a power, a consciousness of the Lord Jesus, a habitual rest in the will of God, which would be a joyful discovery to us; if only we refused to be satisfied with anything less than the full indwelling of the Holy Spirit.

Mr. Spurgeon said once that he never passed a single quarter of an hour in his waking moments without a distinct consciousness of the presence of the Lord. When the Spirit fills the heart, Jesus is vividly real and evidently near. What is He to you? Do you awake in the morning beneath His light touch and spend the hours with Him? Can you frequently look up from your work and perceive His face? Are you constantly seeking from Him power, grace, direction? If He is but a fitful vision, you have not realized the first mark of the gift of Pentecost.

Entire consecration to the service of the Lord Jesus is a great step in advance of the experience of most Christians, but even that is not enough. It is often largely *negative,* but we require something strongly *positive* to meet the necessities of our heart and of our times. And this is to be sought in our entire possession by that mighty Spirit whose advent at Pentecost dated a new era for the church and the world.

Of course He was always in the world. It was the Holy Spirit of Pentecost who brooded over chaos, spoke in prophets and holy men, and gave nerve to the heroes and saints of the Old Testament time. The Day of Pentecost did not introduce a new Spirit into the world, but it inaugurated an era in which the weakest and humblest of the saints might possess Him in the same measure as they did who lived upon its farther side. Before that momentous day, His fullness was the prerogative of only the few, the elite, the Elijahs and Isaiahs and Daniels, but since that day He has been shed forth in all His *plenitude* on *the many*—on women and children; on obscure thinkers and hidden workers; on handmaids and servants; on all and any who were prepared to fulfill the conditions and to abide by the results. Why not on us?

We are willing to admit that the special gifts of the Holy Spirit belong to the apostolic age. Given for a specific purpose, they are now withdrawn; although it is a serious question whether they might not have been continued, if only the church had been more faithful to her sacred trust. But the special gifts of the Holy Spirit are altogether apart from His blessed fullness. That is not the exclusive right of any age. Confined to no limited era or epoch in the history of the church, His fullness pours its tide of light and power around us, as the Nile in flood; and there is not a single plot or garden ground, however remote, into which it will not come, to fertilize and enrich, if only the channel of communication be kept cleansed and open. Alas, that many think that the Almighty, like some bankrupt builder, constructed the portico of His church with marble and has finished it with common brick!

"Be filled with the Spirit" (Ephesians 5:18) is an injunction as wide-reaching in its demands as "Husbands, love your wives" (v. 25), which is found on the same page. It is a positive command, which we must obey for our good, and all God's commands are enablings. In other words, He is prepared to make us what He tells us to become. Moreover, on the Day of Pentecost, in words that are the charter of our right to the fullness of the Holy Spirit, the apostle Peter told the listening crowds that the fullness that had suddenly come on them from the ascended Lord and that was a direct fulfillment of the ancient prophecy was not for them only, or for their children; but for as many as were afar off, even for them whom the Lord God shall call. Are you one of His called ones? Then rejoice because that fullness is for you! Be not faithless, *but believing!* Lay claim at once to the covenanted portion, and thank God for having cast your lot in an age of such marvelous possibilities.

Excite the Holy Desire by Considering What the Fullness of the Spirit Means

We cannot expect to have it if we are quite content to live without it. Our Father is not likely to entrust this priceless gift to those who are indifferent to its possession. Where the flame of desire burns low there can be no intelligent expectation that the Holy Spirit's fullness shall be realized.

And it is not enough to have a fitful and inconstant desire, which flames up today but will remain dormant for months and years. There must be a steady purpose, able to stand the test of waiting (if need be) for ten days and to bear the rebuff of silence or apparent denial.

And yet the flame of desire needs fuel. We must muse before that fire can burn. And it becomes us, therefore, to stir up the gift that is within us by a quiet consideration of all that is meant by becoming Spirit-filled.

There is no book that will so move us in this direction as the Acts of the Apostles. It is perfectly marvelous to see what this fullness did for those who first received it. Cowards became brave. Obtuse intellects that had stumbled at the simplest truths suddenly awoke to apprehend the Master's scheme. Bosoms that had heaved with rivalry and suspicion and desire for earthly power now thought each better than himself and sought to excel in humble ministry to the saints. Such power attended their words that crowds became congregations and Christ's murderers became His worshipers and friends. Councils of clever men were not able to withstand the simple eloquence of indisputable facts. Towns and countries were shaken and yielded converts by the thousands to the unlearned but eager preachers of the Cross.

All this was simply attributable to the power that had become the common property of the whole church. *And there is not a fragment of reason that it should not do so much for us.* As we contrast that triumphant success to our halting progress, shall not we be filled with uncontrollable longings that He should work similar results by us?

We may secure the same results still further by studying the biography of saintly men belonging to recent centuries. Happy the person within reach of a library, the shelves of which are well lined with books of holy biography! He will never be in want of additional stimulus as he reads the stories of McCheyne and W. C. Burns, of Brainerd and Martyn, of Jonathan Edwards and others. He will not envy or repine; but he will constantly lift eye and heart to heaven, asking that as much may be done through himself.

Moreover, the promises of the Scriptures are enough to incite us to the uttermost. Rivers of living water should flow from us. We should never need to be anxious about our words, because they would be given to us; we should be taught all things, and led into the whole circle of truth; we should know Christ, and be changed into His image; we should have power. All this is so fascinating that it is impossible not to glow with a holy desire to be charged with the Holy

Spirit, as a jar with electricity. And, if need be, we shall be prepared to bear the test of long waiting, as the faithful few did in the Upper Room.

Seek This Blessed Fullness from the Right Motive

If you want this fullness that you may realize a certain experience, attract people to yourself, or transform some difficulty into a stepping-stone, you are likely to miss it. You must be set on the one purpose of magnifying the Lord Jesus in your body, whether by life or death. Ask that all inferior motives may be destroyed and that this may burn strong and clear within you.

God will not find water for us to use to turn our own waterwheels. He will do nothing to minister to our pride. He will not give us the Holy Spirit to enable us to gain celebrity, or to procure a name, or to live an easy, self-contented life.

If we seek the Holy Spirit merely for our happiness, or comfort, or liberty of soul, it will be exceedingly unlikely that He will be given. His one passion is *the glory of the Lord Jesus,* and He can only make His abode with those who are willing to be at one with Him in this. "Can two walk together, except they be agreed?" (Amos 3:3). But if you are activated simply by the desire that the Lord Jesus may be magnified in you, whether by life or death; if you long, above all, that men should turn away from you to Him, as they did from John the Baptist, then rejoice, because you are near blessing beyond words to describe. If your motives fall below this standard, trust Him to enlighten and purify them and offer Him a free entrance within. It will not then be long before there shall be a gracious response; and the Lord, whom you seek, shall suddenly come to His temple, and He shall sit as a refiner of silver, that ministers may offer an offering in righteousness (Malachi 3:1–3).

Consider That Holy Scripture Is His Special Organ

A subtle danger besets the teaching of this most helpful doctrine, and it is one that we need to guard against. Some earnest people have magnified the inner light and leading of the Holy Spirit to the neglect of the Word that He gave, and through which He still works on human hearts. This is a great mistake and the prolific parent of all kinds of evil. As soon as we put aside the Word of God, we lay ourselves open to the solicitation of the many voices that speak within our hearts; and we have no test, no criterion of truth, no standard of appeal. How can we know the Spirit of God in some of the more intricate cases that are brought into the court of conscience, unless our judgment is deeply imbued with the Word of God?

We must not be content with the Spirit without the Word, or with the Word without the Spirit. Our life must travel along these two, as the locomotive along the parallel rails. The Word is the chosen organ of the Spirit; and it is only by our devout contact with it that we shall be enabled to detect His voice. It is by the Word that the Spirit will enter our hearts, as the heart of the sun passes into our chambers with the beams of light that enter the open casement.

We need a widespread revival of Bible study. These mines of Scripture, lying beneath the surface, call loudly for investigation and discovery; and those who shall obey the appeal and set themselves to the devout and laborious study of the inner meaning of the Word shall be soon aware that they have received the filling that they seek.

There is no better way of communing with God than to walk to and fro in your room or in the open air, your Bible in hand, meditating on it and turning its precepts and promises into prayer. God walks in the glades of Scripture, as of old He walked in those of Paradise.

Be Prepared to Let the Holy Spirit Do As He Will with You

The Holy Spirit is in us, and by this means Christ is in us; for He dwells in us by the Spirit, as the sun dwells in the world by the means of the atmosphere vibrating with waves of light. But *we must perpetually yield to Him, as water to the containing vessel.* This is not easy; indeed, it can only be accomplished by incessant self-judgment and the perpetual mortification of our own self-life.

What is our position before God in this respect? We have chosen Jesus as our substitute, but have we also chosen Him by the Holy Spirit as our Life? Can we say, like the apostle: "Not I, but Christ liveth in me"? If so, we must be prepared for all that it involves. We must be willing for the principle of the new life to grow at the expense of the *self-life.* We must consent for the one to increase, while the other decreases, through processes that are painful to the flesh. Nay, we must ourselves be ever on the alert, hastening the processes of judgment, condemnation, and crucifixion. We must keep true in our allegiance to the least behest of the Holy Spirit, though it cost tears of blood.

The perpetual filling of the Holy Spirit is only possible to those who obey Him, and who *obey Him in all things.* There is nothing trivial in this life. By the neglect of slight commands, a soul may speedily get out of the sunlit circle and lose the gracious plenitude of Spirit-power. A look, a word, a refusal may suffice to grieve Him in ourselves and to quench Him in others. Count the cost, yet do not shrink back afraid of what He may demand. He is the Spirit of love; and He loves us too well to cause grief, unless there is a reason, which we would approve of if we knew as much as He.

Receive Him by Faith

"As ye have therefore received Christ Jesus the Lord, so walk ye in Him" (Colossians 2:16). Faith is the one law of the divine household. And as once you obtained forgiveness and salvation by faith, so now claim and receive the Holy Spirit's fullness.

Fulfill the conditions already named; wait quietly but definitely before God in prayer, for He gives His Holy Spirit *to them that ask Him;* then reverently appropriate this glorious gift, and rise from your knees and go on your way, reckoning that God has kept His word, and that you are filled with the Spirit. Trust Him day by day to fill you and keep you filled. According to your faith, so shall it be done to you.

There may not be at first the sound of rushing wind, or the coronet of fire, or the sensible feeling of His presence. Do not look for these, any more than the young convert would look to feeling as an evidence of acceptance. But *believe,* in spite of feeling, that you are filled. Say over and over, "I thank You, O my God, that You have kept Your word with me. I opened my mouth, and You filled it, though as yet I am not aware of any special change." And the feeling will sooner or later break in upon your consciousness, and you will rejoice with exceeding great joy; and all the fruits of the Spirit will begin to show themselves.

But Remember It Is Not Enough to Be Filled Once for All

Like the apostles of old, we must seek perpetual refillings. They who were filled in the second chapter of Acts were filled again in the fourth. Happy is that man who never leaves his chamber in the morning without definitely seeking and receiving the plenitude of the Spirit! He shall be a proficient scholar in God's school, for the anointing which he has received, like fresh oil, shall abide in him, and teach him all things. Above all, he will be taught the secret of abiding fellowship with Christ, for it is written, "As [the anointing] hath taught you, ye shall abide in him" (1 John 2:27).

Whenever you are conscious of leakage, when the exhaustion of service has been greater than the reception of fresh supplies, when some new avenue of ministry, freshly discovered talent, or new department of your being has presented itself, go again to the same source for a refilling, a recharging with spiritual power, a re-anointing by the holy baptism.

Three tenses are used in the Acts of the Apostles about the filling of the Spirit, which have their counterparts still:

Filled: a sudden decisive experience for a specific work (Acts 4:8).

Were filled: the imperfect tense, as though the blessed process were always going on (Acts 13:52).

Full: the adjective, indicating the perpetual experience (Acts 6:8).

There is, of course, more in the doctrine of the Holy Spirit than is realized by this writer. The fiery baptism of the Holy Spirit may be something far beyond. Let us not then be content to miss anything possible to redeemed men; but, leaving the things that are behind, let us press on to those before, striving to apprehend all for which we have been apprehended by Christ Jesus.